D0455525

THE MENTAL GAME OF GOLF

THE MENTAL GAME OF GOLF
A Guide to Peak Performance

PATRICK J. COHN, PH.D.

Diamond Communications, Inc.
South Bend, Indiana
1994

THE MENTAL GAME OF GOLF

Copyright © 1994 by Patrick J. Cohn

Manufactured in the United States of America

10 9 8 7 6 5 4 3 2

Diamond Communications, Inc.
Post Office Box 88
South Bend, Indiana 46624-0088
(219) 299-9278
FAX (219) 299-9296

Library of Congress Cataloging-in-Publication Data

Cohn, Patrick J., 1960—
    The mental game of Golf : a guide to peak performance / Patrick J.
Cohn.
        p.   cm.
    Includes bibliographical references.
    ISBN 0-912083-65-4 : $19.95
    1. Golf--Psychological aspects.   I. Title.
GV979.P75C64   1993
796.352--dc20   93-34172
                                                              CIP

DEDICATION

To my sister Audrey M. Cohn, for her generous gift of life. I could not have completed this project without her unselfish sacrifice and continued support.

TABLE OF CONTENTS

ACKNOWLEDGMENTS

I want to thank every golfer who participated in my research projects on *The Mental Game of Golf*, and the players I have worked with who have shared their experiences with me the last few years. I wish to recognize my mentors Dr. Linda Bunker, Dr. Robert Rotella, and Dr. Kenneth Ravizza for sharing their expertise and experience in sport psychology with me. I also greatly appreciate the work of Dr. Peggy Richardson, Gary Battistoni, Hank Schlissburg, and Adam Weinstein for their suggestions on improving the book and providing valued feedback during the writing process.

INTRODUCTION

This is an exciting time in the world of athletics. Progress in science and technology have made possible real advances in athletic training and conditioning, our understanding of diet and nutrition, and high-tech equipment. Athletes today are also realizing that it takes more than physical ability and a well-conditioned body and that they must use both their physical and mental skills to become a champion. Strength, speed, flexibility, timing, and hand-eye coordination are the building blocks, but psychological attributes such as desire, commitment, concentration, trust, and self-control are the vital skills that liberate and sustain superior performances in athletes.

Although there are numerous instructional books, videos, and magazines available for players on how to master the physical game of golf, resources for mastering the mental game of golf are still rare. Young players learn more than they need to know about how to swing a club, but they rarely learn how to master and employ the one thing that guides all behavior: the mind. Players at all levels must have more than a fit body and perfect swing mechanics to excel. A perfect swing is not immune to pressure or mental errors, but a strong mind is.

If you wanted to learn more about how the mind works in golf, who would you ask? Most likely you would ask successful golfers, at all levels, who have mastered the mental game of golf. I have spent the last seven years studying the experiences and the mind of the golfer, learning the challenges for both the amateur and professional player. I discovered that players of all levels must meet the same challenges if they are to play well.

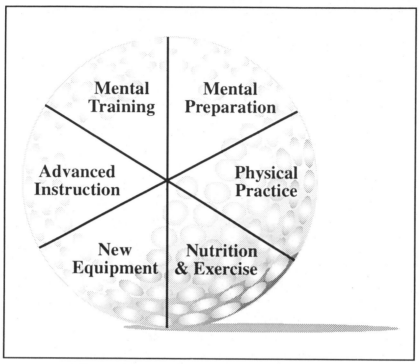

Peak performance requires a holistic approach to the game.

The psychological demands of golf are paradoxical. A player must have determination but not be obsessive, be precise but not perfectionistic, and intense but not overzealous. A player must have high confidence yet be humble, play with self-control but play instinctively, and be focused but not fixated. Finally, a player must be relaxed but not aloof, and play with emotion but not commotion.

Half the battle of the inner game of golf is understanding how the mind works and what thoughts and emotions disrupt even the most mechanically correct swing. Awareness is the key to unlocking one's physical ability, but it is only the first step. The next step is to learn how to use the mind to its full potential.

The focus of this book is about good thinking on the golf course, and what good thinking is. It can help you unlock your physical ability by understanding how the mind can be trained to enhance rather than hinder your performance. This book shows you how to develop a winning attitude, to be happy with your efforts, and to have fun in the process. I hope it will help you become a better and happier player.

I could not have written this book without the knowledge I have gained from studying, working with, talking to, and observing players of all levels. This book will use not only the principles of psychology, but also the actual experiences of exceptional golfers recounting their best performances, to focus on three keys to unlocking potential. The first and foremost is the understanding of how to think effectively on the course and to acquire the mental skills needed to achieve peak performance. The second is learning how to practice effectively off the course to enhance on-course play. Lastly, achieving optimal performance includes tackling the special challenges of golf and gaining a suitable level of commitment and motivation to play your best.

THE PSYCHOLOGICAL
DEMANDS OF GOLF

I was oblivious to the tremendous pressure I was under. I did
not think for a moment of the consequences of a poor shot.
There was no fussing over the technical details of my swing. I
was almost completely unaware of the thousands of people in
the gallery, of the television cameras watching my every
move, of the competitors making a run to overtake me. Mentally and physically it was as though I was on automatic pilot.
My thoughts were clear, ordered, and decisive. All I did was
pull a club from the bag, swing, and the type of shot I envisioned would come off perfectly.
David Graham (1990), PGA Tour,
after winning the 1981 U.S. Open

Moments like these, called playing in the zone, are what all golfers strive for, but they are rare and hard to describe. Playing in the
zone combines superior performance with the highest positive emotions and feelings. Although the ideal is to play consistently in the
zone, the reality is that on most days players only wish they could
find this elusive state.

Golf is a game that is played between the ears. If you ask any
player, amateur or professional, how much of golf is a mental game
they would reply at least 80 percent of golf is mental, after the basic
skills have been learned. Yet, golfers spend countless hours practicing, taking lessons, and reading books to learn how to improve their
swing or putting stroke. Rarely do players spend time improving

1

their mental skills. Why do golfers spend most of their time working on swing mechanics if golf is such a mental game?

The answer is that many golfers don't understand how the mind works and feel more comfortable working on their swing than their attitude. A NCAA champion once said to me: "It is easy to fix a physical problem because I can go to the range and do some drills to correct it, but when it's a mental problem I don't have any drills I can do to correct the problem." This is a result of the lack of emphasis on the mental aspects of golf in books, videos, magazines, and from golf coaches and instructors. Golfers learn that a perfect swing is the secret to having a game that is immune from pressure and mental errors, but a perfect swing is not immune from pressure; the player swinging the club must learn to effectively manage pressure. What most golfers don't know is that there are ways to improve their psychological approach to the game that go beyond learning course management and thinking smart on the golf course.

THE PSYCHOLOGICAL CHALLENGES OF GOLF

Golf is a mental game because it presents unique psychological challenges. Think of the abundant amount of downtime between shots and when waiting for others to play. You spend less than one percent of an 18-hole round actually striking a ball. Unlike athletes in reactive sports, golfers play at their own pace and propel the ball when they are ready to do so. In reactive sports like basketball, soccer, or volleyball the player has less free time and must react to players and a ball almost continually. The downtime in golf presents a challenge to players who analyze and judge their performance. This extra time gives you more time to get "steamed-up" about the last putt you missed, analyze the last hook you hit, or contemplate your next shot.

Golf is the ultimate individual sport. It's you against the golf course. You face the challenges of the golf course alone. There are no teammates to help you or to rely on. You take all the credit when you hit a great shot or when you sink a 30-foot putt. You also accept sole responsibility for hitting a ball out-of-bounds or missing a three-foot putt. On the course there is no place to hide and no teammates to share the blame.

The object of golf and how golf is played presents a contradiction. Hitting a ball that is two and a half inches in diameter with a 36-inch long club with a clubhead four inches in diameter is an incredible task. The game produces perfectionists because of the level of precision, commitment, and desire it takes to become good in golf. The contradiction is that perfectionists try to perfect a game that is impossible to perfect. It's an imperfect game that demands perfection played by imperfect players. Yet, the challenge keeps golfers coming back for more. The better you play, the more you demand of yourself, the easier it is to become frustrated, and the harder it is to accept mistakes.

THE CHARACTERISTICS OF CHAMPIONS

Great athletes must have three attributes to be successful: (1) physical ability; (2) desire, motivation, and commitment; and (3) a strong mental approach to their game. A person can make up for a lack of physical talent with an increase in desire and motivation to work hard and a solid mental approach to the game. In contrast, a player who has good physical talent can play relatively well in spite of a lack of motivation and desire to succeed. The fact is that we are all born with a certain amount of physical ability that cannot be modified through practice. That leaves two areas in which a golfer can improve: motivation and desire, and the mental approach to golf.

Some players are fortunate to be physically talented, but lack the commitment and positive mentality to reach their full potential. Similarly, some players are physically talented and dedicated and committed to their sport, but are also unable to reach their full potential because they lack the mental tools necessary to play their best. To get the most out of your physical ability you have to be a complete player with a strong desire and motivation to succeed and a commitment to understanding the mental game.

Success comes easy for some players, others have to work harder to achieve the same level of success. Some players with less ability than their peers have learned how to use their mind to excel. This type of player exceeds others' expectations because of an intense desire to succeed, a high level of commitment and dedication, and building a mental game that thrives in competition. Although you cannot change your inborn physical ability, you can modify your level of commitment and motivation, and your mental approach to the game.

WHAT'S THE PROBLEM?

There is a common misconception about what a sport psychologist does. Most people think that sport psychologists only work with "mental cases" or problem players, or that sport psychology is only for struggling players. Most of the athletes I work with are healthy persons who want to learn how to cope better with abnormal amounts of stress. Not everyone has a psychological problem that needs fixing. I try to take a positive approach by pointing out that sport psychology helps you become **more** confident, **more** focused, have **more** fun, play **more** relaxed, and know how to practice **more** efficiently. Any player can improve their game even if they don't have a specific problem that needs to be "fixed."

Some players who do have a negative attitude and struggle with their game know they need to make some attitude changes, but don't know how. Others have a poor attitude and struggle on the course, but don't realize that they are crippling themselves with poor thinking. This type of player thinks that degrading oneself, becoming frustrated and anxious are inherent to the game. In my work, half the battle is to make players aware of the ways they sabotage themselves with negative thinking and poor mental "mechanics."

It is difficult for players to know whether an error was due to a mechanical fault, psychological flaw, or both. For many players it's hard to identify the source of a poorly hit shot. Was the slice caused by a purely mechanical problem or were you anxious and hurried your swing? Or was it combination of a mechanical error that was compounded by a lack of confidence? Changing your attitude and mental apporach will not correct a purely mechanical error. First you have to rule out the possibility that you have a mechanical flaw.

How do you tell if an error is psychological or physical? If you hit the ball great on the range and can't seem to take your "practice game" to the course, it is probably psychological. If your errors increase in pressure situations, then it is most likely psychological. When you get mad or frustrated after three putting and sky your next tee shot, it is psychological. If you approach a shot with negative thoughts and images and then hit the ball into the woods, it is psychological.

APPLYING MENTAL TRAINING TO YOUR GAME

We are going to explore the mental game of golf in the following chapters. I offer a method that I hope is broad enough to assist players at all levels, from the high handicap to the professional golfer. The concepts, techniques, and strategies I present are a foundation for improving your game. Of course, it is up to you to make these concepts your own and take them to heart (and mind!) so that you can take them to the course as well.

THE PSYCHOLOGY OF
PEAK PERFORMANCE

> **You get so focused on what you're doing that you don't even know what score you're shooting. At Doral, for example, when I holed that third shot on the eighth hole, I knew I was going to hole it... You just have the ability to make your golf club part of your body. You don't feel your golf swing. You don't get confused by any thoughts. You don't see water out there. You don't see the bunker six or eight feet in front of the pin. I can put a ball within a foot or two of where I am aiming from 183 yards.**
>
> *Greg Norman, in The Zone,*
> *shooting 62 at Doral (Dorman, 1992)*

After thinking about his round, Adam knew it wasn't like normal days. Never before had he felt so confident, no one could beat him that day. There wasn't one shot he couldn't make. He was oblivious to the huge gallery and his playing partners, and so engrossed in playing each shot that the passage of time transcended normal laws. He was amazed how easy and effortless his swing felt, his club was an extension of himself. He didn't have to struggle to execute shots. His thoughts were clear, decisive, and images amazingly vivid. Never before did he feel so in control of his thoughts and emotions. He was in a trance-like state that surpassed the normal limits of functioning. It was so fun to execute each shot as envisioned with such ease and simplicity. Only then did Adam realize that he played the best round of his life, and was "in the zone."

This scenario and when Greg Norman shot 62 at Doral are typical of how players describe a peak performance. Performances like Chip Beck's 59 at the 1991 Las Vegas Invitational and Greg Norman's 62 at Doral are the ultimate achievement in golf. Peak Performance is also referred to as playing in the zone, in the bubble, in a groove, and flow. It is the culmination of a player's combined physical and mental skills and ability.

When in the zone, you play one shot at a time, are totally immersed in each shot, feel highly confident and in control of yourself, and you are fueled by positive emotions. Even the best players in the world play only sporadically in the zone and some players admit they have never played to their potential. Peak performance occurs when your mind and body work in harmony to produce an optimal state of positive emotions and high performance.

Every golfer at one time has had a personal best or has played in the zone for a short period of time. When you play in the zone, several positive emotions and feelings occur, but these emotions also help you play your best. The philosophy of this book is that everyone can learn from the mindset of elite players playing their best golf. When you can lay the foundation for psychological properties associated with playing in the zone, you increase your chances of achieving peak performance. Playing well elicits positive thoughts and emotions and positive thoughts fuel superior performance. When playing in the zone, confidence is high, you're totally focused on the task, you expect good things to happen, and have a lot of fun. A player who is confident, focused, and having fun plays his best.

Positive emotions and thoughts
fuel superior play and
superior play activates
positive emotions and thoughts.

Qualities of Peak Performance

Every player experiences the zone in a unique way, but several universal characteristics occur for all players. Based on research with professional, collegiate, and amateur players and research in sport psychology, this chapter describes the thoughts, feelings and emotions that are typically associated with peak performance.

TOTAL SELF-CONFIDENCE

> **I knew I could play that day. You just feel like you're hitting your shots, you're hitting your targets, you just feel it. It is almost an invincible feeling because you know everything is going your way. I almost won the U.S. Open that day. You see your putts going in. At that point in time your confidence just builds.**
> **Chip Beck, PGA Tour,**
> **1984 U.S. Open (Cohn, 1991)**

The belief in your ability to play well and hit good shots is critical to achieving peak performance. In all sports, self-confidence is the number one psychological quality that separates the champion from the rest of the field. Players constantly attribute their success to a high level of self-confidence in their ability to play well.

Players describe two different types of self-confidence. Self-confidence can be simply thinking that you can win or play well. Self-confidence also can be knowing and trusting that the ball is going to the target or in the hole no matter what. I am sure you feel more confident when hitting a particular type of shot, a shot that you have practiced and successfully executed in the past.

> **Last year [1992] when I shot 63 in Chattanooga the last round, it felt like I ran out of holes because I felt I was going to birdie every hole. That's how much confidence I was playing with. I was attacking every aspect of the game. I was dominating the golf course.**
> **Kelly Gibson, PGA Tour**

Does playing well lead to high self-confidence or does self-confidence help a player play well? Both good play and confidence feed off each other. If you make a few putts early in a round, your confidence with putting grows. Similarly, starting a round feeling

8

confident that you will putt well helps you to make more putts. Most golfers agree that self-confidence is critical to playing your best, but rarely do players work on improving their confidence other than through physical practice. In Chapter 3, I offer several ways besides physical practice to improve your confidence.

"This shot is going straight at the pin."

AUTOMATIC AND EFFORTLESS PERFORMANCE

The less you have to think about, the better... When you just loosen up and let your natural ability do what it can do, you can surprise yourself, instead of trying so hard to make that 40-foot putt go in the hole and really strain and tense-up your muscles, then it doesn't happen.
Cindy Figg-Currier,
LPGA player (Cohn, 1991)

9

A universal ingredient of playing in the zone is a feeling of automatic and effortless execution. Your swing flows with ease. You're in such a groove you feel like you can swing as hard as you like. You don't have to think about the swing and mechanically guide it through its path. Without even trying, you think fade and the ball fades, you think draw and the ball draws.

The swing happens by itself with ease. When in the zone, the swing is spontaneous, simple, and easy. The club becomes an extension of your body and responds to the images that you create. You rely on instincts and let the swing happen naturally based on the swing you have ingrained in practice. One simple swing thought is all that is necessary to initiate the swing, as opposed to having several thoughts in mind when not playing well. PGA Tour player Brandell Chamblee (Cohn, 1991) described the difference between playing well and not playing well:

> **When you are playing well, most of the time you are thinking about one swing thought, you're not thinking about too many mechanical things…and that allows you, in my opinion, to free-up your mind to think about general things like tempo or rhythm. I think when you are playing poorly you have three or four thoughts in your mind.**

Everyone has days when the swing and putting stroke feels in the groove and easy to execute. Your tempo and rhythm feel smooth, ball contact solid, you stroke the ball with less effort, and the ball flies further.

You probably have had days when you didn't play well and everything seemed like a struggle. Your tempo felt uncoordinated. You had too many swing cues competing for your attention at once. The feeling of the ball contacting the club was awkward and the results were inconsistent. In chapter 4, I discuss the importance of learning to let it flow and I help you to learn how to develop a swing that is free of mechanical instructions.

Immersed in the Present Moment on the Task

On the course, I played one shot at a time, one hole at a time,

one round at a time. I was so intent on the job at hand that to this day I cannot remember a single hole on that course.
Amy Alcott (1990), LPGA Tour,
winning in Houston in 1977

Playing in the zone is similar to what Alcott describes. You are highly task-involved and play each shot like it is your only shot. All your mental energy is focused on the task of getting the ball from the tee to green and in the hole in the least number of strokes. Your mind is locked into the target and engrossed in preparing to hit the best shot possible.

You never stop to think about the last putt you lipped-out or the last shot that you didn't hit well. You're so into the present moment that you don't consider what challenges await you in the holes to come. Some players become so process-oriented that they aren't aware of how well they are doing and forget their score. They know they are playing well, but don't stop to think about why and how they're playing so well or about the consequences of playing well.

When immersed in the task, a player focuses all mental energy in the here and now. This means that the player concentrates only on preparing and executing a good shot. A players doesn't concern himself with anything else but club selection, target selection, set-up, and alignment. It is harder to be distracted when you're totally focused. Bob Tway, winner of four tournaments and PGA Tour Player of the Year in 1986, describes how it's difficult to be distracted when playing in the zone:

> I think when you are playing well you're concentrating, you're in the zone. Someone could sound-off a horn in the middle of your swing and you would probably not hear it. If someone dropped a lawn chair, and someone asks, "Did you hear that?" "No, I didn't hear it." You're just focused. And when you are playing bad and not playing as well, man, you are just noticing everything.

When you don't play in the present, your thoughts wander from the immediate task at hand. You recall the six-foot putt you missed on the last hole or you think about difficult holes to come. You start

11

to notice the bunkers and the hazards and it is easier to think about the consequences of hitting a poor shot. In Chapter 5, I talk about immersing yourself in the shot. I discuss what to focus on, how to focus, and how to put your mind in position to score and hit your best shot.

NARROW MENTAL FOCUS

I think with peak performance, the less you have to think about, the better, because you are real focused into that one thing, and that makes it simpler for you and seems to get you into the zone better.
Cindy Figg-Currier, LPGA Tour

Focusing the mind on one specific thought or one external object is another feature of peak performance. A calm, uncluttered mind, is absolutely necessary to play in the zone. Your mind is always active and constantly assessing information, planning a course of action, and carrying on an internal dialogue.

Playing in the zone, you think about the requirements of each shot, plan a course of action, and prepare your body to execute. You calculate the distance to the target, select a club to hit, pick a target, go through your set-up, and only focus on a swing cue or the target. The mind can focus only on one thought or external object at a time without becoming confused, and this is what happens when you're in the zone. E.J. Pfister described his focus when he won the 1988 NCAA Championship:

All I focused on was the ball, the intermediate target, or the pin. And a lot of times when you are playing it is not all that clear. . . it is just really hard to focus on that one point...And that day all I saw was the pin and the middle of the fairway.

When playing in the zone your thoughts are clear, decisive, and uncluttered. When not playing well, you lose that pinpoint focus and struggle with too many thoughts. It's difficult to sort out all the information you are bombarded by in the environment. Your mind becomes cluttered with several swing thoughts at once and it becomes difficult to pull the trigger. You become confused and your swing looses its rhythm and fluidity.

FEELING OF CONTROL

When I'm playing my best golf, I'm in control of everything...You control your fears, you control your level of patience, and you control your confidence level. You don't rush yourself, you find a good pace, a good rhythm. You're not worried about outcomes when in control. When not in control, negative thoughts enter your mind, your playing

partner's mannerisms enter your mind, someone in the gallery might bother you, or your caddie might get under your skin.
Kelly Gibson, PGA Tour

There are several things in golf over which you have no control. The conditions of the course, weather, playing partners, bad bounces, and rulings by officials are a few things that you cannot control, but you can control one thing: how you react and behave. You can't control a bad bounce, but you can control of how you react to that bad bounce when playing.

Controlling your emotions and thoughts is a precondition to playing in the zone. To play well, you can't be frustrated, angry, upset, or anxious when playing. Staying in control of yourself means monitoring your thoughts, keeping your emotions on an even level, staying physically loose in tense situations, and managing your reactions to events beyond your control.

Controlling your thoughts includes thinking about hitting the ball to your target rather than in the water. Controlling your emotions means not letting a missed three-foot putt on the last hole effect your next shot. Control of emotions also includes staying relaxed in pressure situations and not getting upset when your ball comes to rest in a divot. To play in the zone, you must first learn self-control, and be composed especially in situations over which you have no direct control.

When a player is in the zone, it's easy to have self-control because everything is going well, but it's a big challenge to have self-control when not playing well. Making a bad decision about what club to hit or having your ball come to rest in a divot are harder to accept and put behind you when you aren't playing well. It is easier to become frustrated when you miss a two-foot putt for par. You tighten up faster and the tension builds as you try harder to get your game back on track. It is more difficult to release anger after hitting a ball out-of-bounds. The fear of hitting your next tee shot out-of-bounds increases. It is harder to stay in control when things are not going your way, but that is when you have to call upon all your resources to gain control.

In Chapter 6, I discuss how to control your emotions and use adversity and pressure to your advantage.

ABSENCE OF FEAR

I got to the point that where I no longer feared a bad shot, I no longer worried about a bad shot or concerned myself with a bad shot. I just knew at that point in time that I was never going to hit another bad shot that round.
U.S. Club Pro Champion

15

Fear can be one of the most debilitating emotions for all players. More than any emotion, fear can ruin a smooth, relaxed, fluid swing or putting stroke. Fear often is directed to the impending negative consequences of your actions. Playing without fear means not being scared of losing the match, hitting a difficult shot, or being anxious about three-putting. During a peak performance, most golfers would agree that worry about performing badly is overshadowed by the confidence of knowing you will play well. Possible dangerous shots that can evoke strong negative emotions for the golfer who lacks confidence are not present when playing in the zone.

> **When playing well, you always see where you want to hit your shot.**
> *Trevor Dodds, PGA Tour*

When fear dominates your thoughts, it can ruin your performance. The fear of hitting a tee shot out-of-bounds on a tight fairway can cause you to lose confidence, doubt yourself, and tense your muscles. You then start to overcontrol and steer your shots. The fear of missing a three-foot putt for par on the final hole to win the match will certainly cause you to tense up and doubt yourself.

PHYSICAL RELAXATION/MENTAL CALMNESS

> **I think it is very important to learn how to relax because relaxation enables you to stay focused, enables you to continue to do what you did to get yourself in contention. So breathing, stretching, little things you learn help you in those situations.**
> *Bob Tway, PGA Tour*

Think back to when you played your best round. Did you feel physically relaxed, tense, or somewhat between the two? Each of us has an optimal zone of physical readiness or activation that allows us to play our best. Too little or too much activation impairs performance. A lack of intensity can cause you to not have enough energy to make a good swing. Too much excitement can cause you to tighten up and overcontrol the swing. Some players perform their best when they're as relaxed as possible and maintain a calm mind. Other players thrive on a higher level of activation.

To produce a fluid, smooth golf swing or putting stroke, you must be relatively tension free but not so relaxed that the club is too loose in your hands. The muscles work in unison when physically relaxed and this helps you to keep a good pace and rhythm to your swing. Too much physical tension can destroy a fluid and rhythmic swing. Your putting stroke becomes choppy and erratic when you give your putter the death grip and lose the feel of the putter.

Mental calmness is also an important feature of optimal performance. Having a calm or quiet mind is necessary to focus on the task at hand and make sound decisions on the golf course. An overactive, analytical mind becomes cluttered with too much information, which leads to confusion. Have you ever played a round worried about something you have to do after the round? Do you sometimes become confused or paralyzed by too many swing thoughts or mechanical instructions?

Too many task-irrelevant thoughts or internal distractions like mechanical instructions cause your focus to become scattered. In Chapter 6, I discuss the effects of tension on performance and how to find your optimal arousal zone.

ENJOYMENT

> **I love to play this game and work extremely hard at trying to figure out how to play good because I love the chance of winning a tournament, I love the competition, I love the heat of the battle. Those are the rewards I get from practicing. You don't always win, but it is fun to try.**
> *Bob Tway, PGA Tour*

One goal of athletes in all sports is to have a "once in a lifetime" performance. It is an absolute joy to play when everything comes together at once and the mind and the body are working in harmony. On these days, you strike the ball with effortlessness and ease, role putts in unconsciously from everywhere, and feel in total control of the situation. You always feel great as you shoot your best score.

Part of the joy comes from knowing that you played well, but it may also come from beating a tough opponent, attaining a goal, or feeling like you won the battle with yourself and played to your potential. It is fun to experience the feeling of hitting a perfectly hit shot that happened just as you envisioned it. It's fun to make a difficult 40-foot putt that dropped into the center of the cup. You might enjoy appreciating the outdoors and the surroundings or enjoying the company of your playing partners. You feel like savoring the exhilaration of flow and being totally immersed in the activity.

One question that is still a mystery: Do you have fun because you are playing well? Or does enjoying your game help you to play better? The answer is yes to both questions. Did you have fun only after starting to play well and achieve your goals or did you make an effort to have fun playing before you tee-off? Cindy Figg-Currier said that playing well and fun go hand in hand:

> **Your objective is to play good and win, but if you can do that having fun——that is the ultimate. So one complements the other, you make a few good putts you're having fun and if you are having fun you can play well.**

FINAL THOUGHTS ON PEAK PERFORMANCE

Playing in the zone does not occur often. But it is an ideal state of mind for which all players strive. The best players in the world rarely, if ever, play in the zone for four straight rounds. How often have you been able to get into the zone and play to your physical limit? It comes and it goes; you can't make yourself suddenly find the zone, and you don't know when it will happen. You can lay the groundwork for playing at your peak, but then you must let it happen. PGA Tour player Kelly Gibson describes how hard it is to predict when he will find the zone:

> **The big problem with getting into the zone is unfortunately you can't predict when you're going to do it. It's not like other sports where you can peak your training so that you're ready for that particular track meet or football game.**

On most days, players shoot within a range of below average to above average. Once a player breaks 80, he expects to be able to repeat that level of play every day, which is very hard to do. A tour player who shoots 65 the first day of a tournament is upset with a less-than-perfect round of 70 the next day. It is easy to compare every round to your previous best round, but this can lead to frustration and disappointment. The goal is to play consistently better, but not always in the zone.

Some players evaluate a less-than-perfect round as a failure. They trap themselves into a pattern of thinking called the "all or none syndrome." These players look back on their last performance and judge it as either good or poor, with nothing in between. This type of thinking can sap motivation and doesn't allow you to evaluate your play honestly. More often than not, your performance may not match or even come close to your expectations. Thinking that anything less than your best round is a failure can cause you to judge yourself negatively, feel unsatisfied, and lose motivation.

You also must realize that there are some things that you cannot control on the golf course. There is a certain amount of luck that goes into playing well or playing poorly. Sometimes you get an unlucky break, sometimes you get a lucky one. You may hit a shot next to the pin, but it hits a hard spot and rolls off the green. You may hit a great shot and have it turn out poorly, or you may hit a poor shot and it turns out well.

> **You can hit a great shot and end up 10 or 15 feet from the hole, or you can hit a lousy shot and it goes in the hole, and that's just the nature of golf.**
> *David Edwards, four-time winner on the PGA Tour*

Learning to play in the zone is important to achieving peak performance in golf, but "zoning" is the final icing on the cake. To play your best requires more than being confident, focused, and free on the golf course. Achieving peak performance requires that you have the dedication, commitment, and hard work that lay the groundwork for playing in the zone. Without the desire to play your best, without commitment to working hard, and without the physical and mental preparation to give you confidence, you cannot truly play to your potential.

In the next few chapters I discuss each of the psychological qualities of playing in the zone and how you can build a foundation for playing in the zone more consistently. Although you

19

can't consciously make yourself play in the zone, you can certainly set the groundwork with appropriate thoughts, feelings, and emotions that will increase your chances of finding the zone and achieving peak performance.

The last two chapters discuss the importance of quality practice and practicing in a way that helps you play your best on the course, and the importance of finding the right level of motivation and commitment for you to excel in golf.

CONFIDENCE: THE KEY TO OPTIMAL PERFORMANCE

I think confidence is very important. I think it is important for everybody. Anybody who plays good, their confidence is high, there's no doubt about it. It makes you more relaxed and you're able to let the golf swing just happen. If you're a little bit anxious, nervous, apprehensive about something, you cut your swing off, get quick, you don't enable yourself to flow through the swing.
Bob Tway, PGA Tour

High self-confidence is the most important psychological quality to possess in any sport. Coaches, athletes, and sport psychologists agree that confidence is the key to consistently high performance. Like Bob Tway, athletes from all sports attribute optimal performance to a persistent belief in themselves and their ability. Self-confidence is even more important in golf where you are the only person responsible for the final score.

Athletes who play with high self-confidence are more relaxed, and don't get scared, intimidated, or anxious. Athletes with high confidence focus on the positive, maintain optimistic thoughts, and allow themselves to trust their ability in crucial situations. High self-confidence is critical for winning in golf. Even if your mechanics don't feel perfect, confidence allows you to win because you feel so strongly that you can do it.

I won four times in one year. You can win when you're not even playing good because you are very confident.
Bob Tway, PGA Tour

Confidence is talked about often, yet little is known about where it comes from and how it is acquired or lost. One day you may be overflowing with it and the next day have a shortage. What makes confidence so elusive and irregular? If confidence is the backbone to success in sport, then why is so little attention devoted to developing confidence? Most athletes falsely assume that it can only be gained through success or good play, and beyond playing well, they can't control it. Success does play an important part, as David Edwards said: "I don't go play with confidence without a history to base that confidence on." Yet many athletes have high confidence in themselves regardless of the amount of success they experience.

This chapter defines self-confidence from the golfer's perspective. Then, I discuss the origin of self-confidence, how it is gained, and how it is destroyed. Lastly, I present ways to help you learn to improve and maintain your self-confidence.

WHAT IS SELF-CONFIDENCE?

Self-confidence means different things to different people. In general, high confidence is the strong belief you have in your ability to get the job done. It is a belief of how well you think you will play. A belief in your ability can be both general and specific. The belief in your ability to play well or be successful is one way to look at confidence. More specifically, confidence is the belief in your ability to hit a good shot or sink a putt in a given situation. Confident players think they are the best player in the tournament and can win. Confident players also feel they "can do just about anything" given their skill level. Regardless of how you define it, confidence is the true belief you have about how well you can or will play.

WHERE DOES CONFIDENCE COME FROM? HOW IS IT GAINED?

The belief that success breeds confidence and confidence breeds success is undoubtedly true in any sport. The more success you experience and the better you perform, the higher your belief in yourself. Many professional players feel like they can win any tournament they play based on their record of success. Winning a tournament, competing at a higher level of competition, or attaining personal goals all contribute to your belief in your ability to play.

Self-confidence is vital to achieving peak performance at any level. If you have played well in the past and think you can play well, most likely you will. You may not be able to directly control the amount of success you attain, but you can control how confident you feel.

Quality practice can be an immediate and primary source for developing self-confidence. For most athletes, quality practice is needed to gain confidence in their sport. D.A. Weibring, three-time winner on the PGA Tour, gains confidence from dedicating himself to preparing and practicing to the best of his ability:

> **To me, when I know that I've put the time in and worked hard and I've committed myself... like I went back and did all those things these past 10 days to prepare... that gives me confidence that I'm on the right track.**

To trust that you can fade a ball into a green, you must first work at fading the ball in practice to trust that skill when you play. To feel comfortable about what you can do, you need to have put in the necessary time and "paid the dues."

Some athletes rely less on practice and hard work and more on their talent or ability to gain confidence. Talented athletes know that they have the ability to be successful in their sport. Trusting that your ability helps you attain any goal is a tremendous and enduring source of belief, which indeed is the definition of self-confidence. The problem is that not all persons are lucky enough to be endowed with great physical talent.

> **The harder you prepare for anything, the higher your level of confidence about it, thus the less pressure you feel, thus the better you perform.**
> *Seve Ballesteros (1988), PGA Tour*

Confidence also can be attained from significant others in your life. Many players gain trust in themselves from interactions with other persons such as coaches, friends, family, or other players. Your coach showing belief in you, other players complimenting and praising you, and family members supporting you can all have a positive influence on self-confidence. When other persons show you respect, expect you to play well, and always tell you how good you are, you start to feel confident. A survey of PGA Tour players was conducted in 1991 asking who had the best swing on the tour. The players voted Tom Purtzer as having one of three of the best swings on tour. When asked what he thought about the results of the survey, Purtzer said that it gave him "a boost of confidence."

Two other areas impact your belief in your ability: the specific situations you encounter on the course and knowledge about yourself and the game. First, there are many situations you encounter daily that may potentially increase your confidence. Playing a course that suits your game, making a few putts in a row, playing well under pressure, and beating a strong opponent can all boost your self-confidence. For example, Ian Baker Finch shot a course record 64 during the third round of the 1991 British Open before going on to win the tournament. Baker Finch's trust peaked after making a few putts early in the round:

> **The start is what got me going. I made a good 20-foot putt at the second hole, a six-footer at the third, a six-footer for par at the fourth, and another 20-footer for birdie at the fifth. So those four holes in a row gave me the feeling that I could make the putts. Even though I missed a couple of short putts later on, the confidence was still high from holing those putts earlier in the round.**

Knowledge about yourself and the game also can be a foundation for developing a strong inner belief. For example, understanding the mechanics of the golf swing and how to repeat a consistent swing can lead to high self-trust for some golfers.

Thus, there are many sources of confidence and every player gains confidence differently. Some players gain confidence from practicing, others from believing in their talent. Some players gain confidence from winning a tournament, others from hitting a good shot or playing a course that is suited to their game. The thoughts and feelings you have about yourself and your game also influences your level of confidence.

Where do you derive self-confidence? What is the pattern for your development of self-conviction? Do you gain more belief from your talent or past success, or from hitting a good shot or playing well during a round? Is the belief in yourself influenced more by external factors (other persons or events), or is it swayed more by internal factors (belief in talent or thoughts you maintain)?

WHAT HURTS CONFIDENCE? HOW IS IT DESTROYED?

Self-confidence is sometimes destroyed much faster than it develops. Just as playing well can help, poor play can hurt confidence. Some golfers base their belief in their ability on how solidly they hit the ball, how many putts they make, and how low they score. As the players's self-trust declines from playing poorly, their game gets even worse and their trust deteriorates further; it is a vicious cycle.

The ways you gain confidence can potentially work against you. Three-putting the first green, playing in poor weather, and playing a course that doesn't suit your game are examples of competitive situations that may ruin trust. If you depend on a good warm-up to feel comfortable with your game, what happens when you can't practice or when the practice session doesn't fulfill your idea of good practice. Golfers who base confidence on how well the ball is hit in practice and have a poor warm-up prior to the round are likely to play poorly. Golfers who constantly compare themselves to other more skilled players begin to doubt themselves. Also, players who depend on others for feeling poised are susceptible to feeling apprehensive when the support from others is taken away.

For some players, missing one putt in a critical situation ruins confidence to the point that it takes weeks or even months to build it back. Not many people recall when Seve Ballesteros got knocked out of the first playoff hole at the 1987 Masters when he three-putted the 10th green. Everyone focused on Larry Mize when he chipped in to beat Greg Norman in the playoff. Ballesteros confessed later that he took almost two years to regain his self-assurance with his short putts after three-putting the first playoff hole. For most players, confidence usually is destroyed during a slump or over a long period when they are not playing well.

> **When you are confident, you don't even have to be playing that well, because you're so relaxed and swinging so smoothly, your misses are not too bad. Even if you feel like you're playing good but don't have too much confidence, you still get quick and your shots are worse than they should be.**
> *Bob Tway, PGA Tour*

ENDURING, LONG-TERM, SELF-EMPOWERED SELF-CONFIDENCE

There is no substitute for consistent quality practice, sustained success, and a positive attitude. Seeing small improvements in your game through regular practice, repeatedly experiencing success in your sport, and perceiving events in a healthy way are the foundation for a long-lasting high level of confidence. There are also "quick fix" methods that can boost your self-conviction. The ultimate confidence is a stable, long-lasting, high self-confidence that perseveres through any circumstance.

TUNE INTO YOUR PATTERNS

There is not one method for gaining confidence. Everybody acquires and gains confidence differently. What ways do you gain or lose self-confidence? What are the events or thoughts and feelings that can potentially hurt your confidence? Also, contrast the thoughts and feelings you have when performing with maximum confidence with the thoughts and feeling you have when playing with low confidence. The first step to gaining confidence is to examine the thoughts, feelings, and situations that help you gain confidence, and what it feels like to play with high confidence. Armed with this information, you can focus on methods of gaining trust that are more relevant for you.

TAKE CONTROL, DON'T BE CONTROLLED

Your confidence can be influenced by circumstances beyond

your control. Have you ever felt before a round that you would not play well because the greens were in pathetic condition? Do you ever feel intimidated when you played a course that you did not like or didn't suit your game? When you allow a situation to intimidate you, it dictates how much confidence you play with during the round. Don't let challenging situations scare you and cause you to doubt your ability.

Don't let the course intimidate you, you intimidate the course with your shot-making abilities.
Kelly Gibson, PGA Tour

Some situations can have a positive effect on your confidence. Playing a course or playing in weather conditions that you like, and playing on greens that are suited to your game are situations that you can benefit from. It may sound like a contradiction to say, if the situation helps to give you an edge, use it to your advantage—if the situation hinders you from getting what you want, learn to downplay it—but you have to think in ways that help and not hurt you.

I worked with a college golfer at the University of Virginia who liked to play when it was windy. He hit the ball very low and played better than most people in the wind. The harder the wind was blowing, the more confident he felt because he believed he had an advantage over other players. Use any situation or thought you can to help boost your confidence. But the best way is to be confident in your ability regardless of the circumstances you encounter.

Your task is to decide what things are within your control that can significantly impact your confidence. You're in charge of the amount and quality of your practice. How you respond to three-putting is under your control. You control the mental and physical preparation you do. You decide what to focus on and what to think in a given situation. What ways can you increase your self-trust that are within your power? Direct your attention to the methods that are within your control.

Develop Long-Lasting and Enduring Confidence

One bad shot can ruin confidence that has been built up over months or years. Many players' confidence varies from moment to moment depending on the situation, but not if it is true confidence. I have discovered two kinds of confidence in golf. The first is based on experiences such as past success, good play, healthy practice, and a lifetime of training. I call this "enduring confidence" because it is stable, more consistent, and based on long-term factors. The second kind is confidence that changes when you hit your first bad shot or first three-putt. This type of confidence changes with the difficulty of your next shot or how good the last shot was hit. It is more erratic and fragile, and changes from moment to moment during play.

Situational confidence is prone to fluctuate with the demands of each shot. Hitting a shot with a club you're not comfortable with, playing a hole that does not suit your style of play, and hitting a bad shot are examples of specific events that influence your thought patterns at any given moment. This type of confidence is fragile and inconsistent. When you have high enduring confidence, you approach situations on the golf course with high confidence despite the circumstances. David Edwards has confidence that is based on years of consistent play on tour. His confidence doesn't vary greatly from one day to the next or from one shot to the next:

> **Confidence is something that changes slowly—It doesn't go up and down in one day—you play good one day, you play bad the next day. That, to me, is not confidence. Confidence happens over a long period of time. As I look back and say I played the tour for 14 years there is a certain amount of confidence that's gained from that performance over a period of time... a belief that you maintained for a period of time, you'll probably maintain that.**

Thus, it is important to develop stable, long-lasting trust, which is not influenced by how well you're playing or what course your playing. This means developing a belief in your ability that is founded on long-term factors like past success, overcoming adversity, hours and hours of practice, and your ability level. Recall how much you have practiced and remember you have "paid the dues" that are necessary to compete at your level. This is an excellent example of anchoring your confidence in something that cannot be taken away from you.

Feed off of the past by remembering you have paid the dues and have earned the right to be confident in that situation.

When you confront a long shot over water, recall similar shots you hit successfully in the past, in practice, and in competition, rather than letting a single event cause you to be indecisive and doubt yourself about playing that shot.

HIGH CONFIDENCE, NOT FAKE CONFIDENCE

You cannot have too much belief if it is based on reality. A feeling of being too sure of yourself can be a scary experience even in those times when you are playing in the zone and everything feels so good that you think you can do just about anything. You can't be too self-assured about playing well or hitting a good shot if your belief is honestly based on your level of skill.

You can have fake confidence. Fake confidence is believing you can do something that is truly above the range of your physical abilities or skills. It is feeling that you can execute a shot that you have never practiced instead of realizing that you are not competent to hit the shot. Fake confidence is like the golfer who erroneously thinks she can hit a hook around a tree without ever having attempted the shot before in practice or competition. It is simply believing you are a better player than you really are.

> **When people ask me how I'm able to play with such boldness and assurance, I give them only one answer: I know exactly what my skills are and I trust them...Knowledge and understanding of my game have brought an inner confidence and perspective.**
> *Greg Norman (1988), PGA Tour*

Being too self-assured may introduce other problems when you don't keep things in perspective. Overconfidence is destructive when you start to think that you can't improve. You begin to believe that practice is unnecessary and you stop practicing. Overconfidence also can make you think that there is no need to listen to the sound advice of others, like from a friend, coach, or sport psychologist. Overconfidence also can lead to failure to prepare fully for competition.

*Real self-confidence is a strong belief
in your ability to play without
overstating your present skill level.*

True self-confidence is an unyielding inner belief in your ability without exaggeration of how good you are or the skills you possess. It is an understanding of your upper limits of ability, skill level, or competence, and not exceeding that limit. You can't be too self-assured if it is based on reality and not illusion, and if it doesn't lead to problems with motivation to practice and improve.

THINK, FEEL, AND ACT CONFIDENT

True confidence must be earned. It is developed by seeing small improvements in performance, practicing on a regular basis, and developing competence in your skills. Even then there are times when you doubt yourself. You must then do something to boost confidence immediately. Even professionals can lose their belief despite the success they have experienced. Maintaining optimistic thoughts and feeling and acting poised is one way to maintain your belief in yourself during times of adversity.

Confidence is heavily influenced by the thoughts you maintain. You can only hurt your performance by negative thinking, doubt, indecision, and fear. Everyone has different thoughts about their ability. What do you think about when you feel totally confident? Do you believe you can hit your target or make the putt, or do you think the last poor shot you hit was a fluke? Recapture the thoughts you had when you felt poised and composed in order to boost your confidence when it's low.

*You must think, feel, and act
like the ball is going in the
hole to give yourself the
best chance of making the putt.*

Thinking positively doesn't mean convincing yourself that you can hit a shot when you truly know you can't. Positive thinking means giving yourself the best chance to hit a good shot by thinking in a healthy way rather than becoming overpowered by doubt and indecision. Positive thinking is not pumping yourself up with false confidence. The intention is to send signals to yourself that you have what it takes rather than succumbing to fear or doubt. You run the show, don't wait to hit a good shot before you start to feel confident.

Thinking confidently is one piece of the pie. Thinking, feeling, and acting confident is the entire package. What do you feel when you are totally self-assured? How do you act or behave when you feel you can't lose? Your thoughts should conform to your behavior and feelings, and vice versa. Thinking you can sink a long putt and then hoping that it stops near the hole so you can two-putt is an example of thoughts and actions out of harmony. Acting confidently should be backed up with the appropriate thoughts and feelings. True confidence is supported with the corresponding thoughts, feelings, and actions. Think optimistically and maintain positive feelings and appropriate actions to support your thoughts.

BE ACCOUNTABLE, DON'T DELAY

Many amateur golfers let their level of play influence their confidence. If you wait to become confident until after you play well on the first few holes, this becomes an error in mental preparation. Why wait until you hit the first solid shot or make the first putt to start to feel confident? If you have to wait until you hit a good shot to be confident, what happens when your warm-up did not go well or if you hook or slice your first tee shot?

Ultimate self-confidence is
believing in yourself all the
time regardless of whether you
are 10 over par or two under par.

To play well, be accountable for playing with confidence before you tee it up. Performance is too erratic when you begin to doubt your ability because of the last putt you missed. Too many factors that you cannot control can influence the outcome of a putt or a shot. Your confidence starts from within and works outward rather than from the outside in. Don't delay an important part of your mental preparation. Work on improving your enduring confidence, prepare to be confident, and do what it takes to keep it high.

YOU GET WHAT YOU EXPECT TO GET

The saying "you get what you expect" is certainly true about your attitude on the golf course. Confidence is partly an expectation about how well you think you will play. But success is blocked by the belief that you won't succeed. You need to imagine success or picture in your mind what you want rather than what you fear. How can you improve trust in yourself if you are always looking for reasons why you're not going to play well, doubting your ability to play well, or fearing the negative consequences of your actions?

Imagining success means looking for reasons to play well rather than reasons to play poorly, expecting good things to come rather than fearing what might go wrong, and seeing yourself playing well rather than expecting to make mistakes and playing poorly.

An excellent example of expecting good things to happen is when Greg Norman chipped in for an eagle on the first playoff hole at the 1990 Doral Open to beat Simpson, Azinger, and Calcavecchia in a sudden death playoff. After Norman won he said: "I was lining up my chip and Bruce [his caddie] said, 'Chip it in, you're due.' I said, 'OK, sure,' he gave me that extra shot of confidence I needed." (Van Sickle, 1990).

In psychology, the concept of getting what you expect is called the self-fulfilling prophecy. For example, if you think that you are a poor putter and are always looking for reasons to support this belief, then your performance follows your suggestion and you never putt well. Give yourself the best chance of being successful, like Greg Norman did with a great chip shot, envision what you want to have happen not what you fear could happen.

Negative mental images increases anxiety and programs yourself for failure.

PREPARE TO BE CONFIDENT

One way to gain confidence is to put in the preparation and the time necessary to be confident when you tee-it-up. There are several ways to prepare yourself and increase your confidence for a tournament. Doing your homework and knowing you can pass the test is a great source of confidence. Obviously, physical practice is a good foundation for confidence. Other ways to prepare to be confident include making sure you have the right equipment, studying the course by checking yardages, creating a game plan to attack the course, and mentally preparing for any situation that you may encounter. D.A. Weibring feels that preparation and organization are the key to feeling ready to play:

I'm a big believer in good preparation and organization no matter if it's off the golf course in business affairs or if it's getting prepared in playing a golf tournament. I always feel good when I add the appropriate time to practice and put my game in shape before I get to the golf tournament.

UPHOLD HEALTHY PERCEPTIONS

The ability to perceive and interpret events in your life so as to give yourself the best chance of playing well is an important ingredient to achieving peak performance. Perceptions are like filters that color what you see and experience in life. Perceptions influence what you see, and how you think and interpret daily life occurrences.

Hitting a good shot can be interpreted both positively and negatively. Sinking a putt for a birdie can be viewed negatively if you felt you were lucky and didn't make a birdie the "right way." Likewise, playing a difficult course can be perceived as positive or negative, depending on your interpretation. Your perceptions are colored by your combined life experiences and how you integrate those experiences into your stream of consciousness.

Negative thinkers color positive events in a self-destructive manner by focusing only on what went wrong or what should have or could have been better. After a good round, negative thinkers remember the two or three bad shots they hit or the putts they missed, discounting all the other shots that were played well. I often hear golfers say, "It could have been a great round if only I hadn't missed those two short putts for birdie." Positive thinkers focus on what went well and how they can become better. Positive players choose to think about all the great shots, accepting the poor shots as an accident.

If you're going to succeed, you have to feed off the positives.
Tom Kite (1990), PGA Tour

Take the example of playing in poor weather. A negative thinker sees rainy weather as an excuse to play poorly. He searches for a reason for why he can't play well and is unhappy when it rains, which sets him up for failure before he starts. Positive players know everybody has to play in the same conditions and view it as an opportunity to play well. These players perceive the situation in a healthy way by thinking that they have an edge over players who become frustrated in poor weather.

In golf, failure is inevitable and you lose much more often that you win. This requires you to perceive situations in a way that helps your self-confidence. Keep focused on positive elements and view adversity and challenges as an opportunity to get better and learn. A good example of interpreting adversity as a positive experience is Greg Norman, who lost in the 1986 PGA Championship when Bob Tway holed a bunker shot for the win. Norman was disappointed, but he was satisfied with his performance. He was determined to not let one shot from another player ruin his confidence. One year later Norman faced a similar situation in the 1987 Masters when Mize chipped in a 100-foot shot to beat him:

> **"I'm confident that my disappointment at Augusta will ultimately have the same positive effect that my other near misses have had...But through those disappointments I learned a lot. I learned that I am a good enough player to lead all four majors in a single year, and to hold a share of the final-round lead in five majors in a row. And if I can lead them during those final rounds, certainly I can lead them after the tournaments are over. All four of them. In the same year. Yes, I learned I am capable of winning the Grand Slam." (Norman & Peper, 1988)**

There are many things you can't control in golf, like the weather, your opponents, or the conditions of the course. But you do have control over how you think, feel, act and respond in any situation. An important question you should continuously ask yourself is: Am I thinking positively and strengthening my self-confidence so I can get what I truly want?

ONWARD AND UPWARD

In conclusion, you develop true self-confidence from past accomplishments, preparing to be confident, and improving your

37

skills. When you base your confidence on things that are within your control like practice, trusting your skills, maintaining positive thoughts, and making improvements in your game, self-confidence can flourish. Genuine self-belief is long-lasting, enduring, and does not significantly change from moment to moment. Your challenge is to think positive thoughts, feel and act confidently, and expect to play well when you begin to get scared or start to doubt yourself. Don't delay an important part of your mental preparation by waiting for something good to happen before you feel secure. You are the only person responsible for staying positive and sustaining healthy perceptions about your game. Envision what you want to accomplish. Instead of thinking that you must first be able to achieve before you can believe in yourself, try thinking that you must first be able to believe before you can achieve.

CHAPTER SUMMARY

• Assess the way that you gain and lose confidence. What ways can you improve your confidence that are under your control?

• Don't allow the circumstances you have no control over, such as course conditions, weather conditions, playing partners, and so on, influence how confidently you play.

• Base your confidence on enduring qualities like ability, talent, practice, and past success so your confidence is not prone to the yo-yo syndrome.

• You can't have too much confidence about making a shot if your confidence is rooted in a genuine assessment of your present skill level.

• When you're not playing with complete confidence, sometimes you have to fake it until you can gain it. Think, feel, and act like you are confident until you begin to get confident.

• Don't wait until you hit your first good shot to feel comfortable about your ball striking. Prepare to be confident and be confident in your preparation.

• You get what you expect. Expect good things to happen and reasons to play well rather than looking for reasons to fail and expecting to play poorly.

• Interpret events in a way that helps you believe in yourself and your ability. Pick out the positive in a negative situation and don't downplay positive experiences.

LEARN TO LET
IT FLOW

You can't be thinking about eight different things. You've got to pick your target, make your decision, trust it, and go.
D.A. Weibring, PGA Tour

What works well is to almost have a clean slate, don't really be thinking of a lot of stuff. The more you think about, the worse you are sometimes.
David Edwards, PGA Tour

Swinging freely without consciously directing your shots or putts is critical to peak performance in golf. One major quality of peak performance is having the feeling of swinging automatically, which has been described as "in the groove," instinctive, natural, flowing, and effortless. Developing an automatic and effortless swing is essential for superior performance at all skill levels. Most professional golfers agree that an uncluttered mind free of technical instructions is essential to peak performance in golf.

The feeling of an effortless and unmechanical swing results from plenty of practice. One purpose of practice is to develop a movement pattern that repeats itself by simply "pulling the trigger" to start the motion. Playing unconsciously requires learning the fundamentals of the swing and putting stroke with the desire and persistence to produce repeatability. Just as important to developing an automatic swing is how you practice. This chapter discusses the mechanisms that allow you to learn how to swing unconsciously with the feeling of ease and provides a rationale for the importance of learning to "let it flow." Later, I present how to develop an automatic and effortless swing.

> **The golf swing happens far too fast for you to direct your muscles consciously. Frequently I can make minor adjustments in midswing, but they are always instinctive, never conscious.**
> *Jack Nicklaus (1974), PGA Tour*

THE LEARNING PROCESS: MAKING IT AUTOMATIC

Grooving an automatic swing follows a lot of practice and more practice. All physical skills develop in stages before you reach the final point of automatic, subconscious execution. Although you may have a well-learned swing that is repeatable, this section helps you understand the difference between playing mechanically and playing instinctively, and the process that allows you to put it on automatic pilot and swing freely.

Attempting to learn a new skill is never natural at first. Take putting for example. You started by learning the fundamentals of how to stroke the ball. You were instructed (or you experimented) on the grip, set-up, posture, alignment, and putting stroke. Early in learning, you were training your body "how to" perform the stroke, which required you to focus on the technical aspects of the stroke. During the early stage of learning, the mind controlled your muscles directly. Soon, you learned to putt with the help of an instructor or by trial and error.

Initially you had to attend to the mechanics of the stroke. As you refined your stroke, it didn't require as much conscious direction to hit the putt. Midway through the learning process, you made small adjustments in technique to adjust your putting to your idea of a good stroke. The mind was less focused on mechanics, but you needed to focus on technique and consciously control your muscles to make small changes in the stroke, such as thinking about accelerating through the ball. Your feel for a "correct" stroke was beginning to become ingrained in your mind, allowing you to recognize the feeling of a poor stroke.

After going through a process of making small adjustments, you entered the final stage of learning. You started executing the swing without consciously directing your muscles. You grooved a repeatable swing; no longer did you have to think about "accelerating through the ball," it became natural with practice. You felt it when you made a poor stroke and adjusted easily without much practice. You put your mind in neutral while your subconscious executed the swing; the stroke happened all by itself. A simple trigger or swing cue started the stroke in motion. This freed your conscious mind to think about the line of the putt or to visualize the ball rolling into the cup.

All motor skills are learned by first controlling the movement, and eventually skills become ingrained in memory. Most professionals have developed an unmechanized free-flowing style of putting. For example, Seve Ballesteros learned to use a trigger to begin his stroke and then let it happen:

> **Once I feel ready to go, I trigger the back swing by gently pulling the club away from the ball with my right hand, after which my feeling of the stroking motion is essentially that it "just happens." I never feel as if I am ever forcing any part of the stroke. (Ballesteros, 1988)**

A great deal of practice is necessary to reach this stage of automaticity. As you practice, you develop a stronger swing "memory pattern" in your mind (called "muscle memory" by others). Having a strong memory pattern allows you to feel confident that you can hit the shot you call upon from memory. Learning to let it flow not only requires hours and hours of practice, but that practice must also be used to facilitate the automatic execution of the swing. Even when you have a seemingly natural swing, you can interfere with it in many ways. Mechanical, consciously controlled practice is necessary early in the learning process or when making a major swing change. The paradox is that once your swing has become well learned, being mechanical and cognitively controlling your swing is counterproductive to peak performance.

BARRIERS TO LEARNING TO LETTING IT FLOW

If physical practice were the sure road to grooving an automated swing, then with enough time everyone would have an effortless, repeatable swing. But physical practice alone is not the answer. You can interfere with your ability to let it flow by the way you practice and by maintaining self-limiting beliefs or habits. This section describes the self-defeating habits, attitudes, and myths that restrict you from letting it flow. The four major blocks to letting it flow are (1) practicing golf rather than playing golf; (2) over concern with the mechanical side of golf; (3) inability to trust your swing; and (4) perfectionistic tendencies.

PRACTICING GOLF RATHER THAN PLAYING GOLF

One major barrier to freeing it up when it comes time to play is getting stuck in the practice trap. The practice trap is an attitude that thinks you must practice to improve technique only. This attitude does not allow you to play golf because you never enter the final stage of learning the swing. Working on swing mechanics is necessary to become a better golfer. The problem is when practicing to perfect your technique becomes more important than scoring well, you never make the transition from controlling your swing to letting it flow.

Many golfers cannot get out of the practice mode, which is counterproductive to scoring well.

Golfers who get caught in the practice trap have a difficult time playing golf; they practice golf. Golfers who practice golf and always work on their swing never learn to free themselves and score well. They are consumed with perfecting the mechanics and look of the swing, which leads to poor scoring.

OVEREMPHASIS ON MECHANICS

Developing perfect technique is an honorable goal but this blocks your ability to let it flow. The compulsive behavior of always changing your mechanics is fostered by the fact that approximately

95 percent of golf instruction (including books and magazines) deals with mechanics of the swing or putting stroke. Everyone has a different philosophy about how the swing should look, how it should be taught, and the best way to learn. The overemphasis on mechanics in the world of golf leads to a belief that more is better and your swing should conform to the ideal swing.

> **If you're analyzing every shot for mechanical flaws, sooner or later you're going to find some and it's going to be very difficult for you to trust.**
> *Tom Kite (1990), PGA Tour*

Coaches and golf instructors are well known for instilling this type of attitude. What do instructors usually do? They look at your swing, diagnose a flaw or an area to improve, and then break the swing down into parts to be worked on. This is a necessary process for making changes or improvements; to improve your game it is true that you must analyze, identify faults and make appropriate corrections.

The problem starts when you don't stop analyzing, breaking down, and working on the swing at the most critical time--when playing golf. You never learn to trust your swing if your swing is in a constant state of transformation. You become locked in the habit of constantly analyzing your swing or putting stroke and how to improve your technique and this is counterproductive to grooving an automatic swing. Rarely do coaches instruct students to develop mental skills such as developing a good pre-shot routine or acquiring trust in the swing.

Constantly analyzing and changing your technique usually leads to "paralysis by overanalysis." When you always analyze, judge, or evaluate your swing, it is difficult to swing freely. You overcontrol your swing instead of letting a well-grooved swing to run its course automatically.

> **When your in the zone, you can see things easier, like with putts, you can see the line better. But more than anything you are a lot more freer and you just hit it...And so those things happen when you just let it go and start with a good attitude to begin with.**
> *Cindy Figg-Currier, LPGA Tour*

Too many verbal instructions cause you to overcontrol the shot.

Even a world class player such as Seve Ballesteros can get caught up in the mechanics and forget how to get the ball in the hole. In 1989 he forgot his policy. In an interview with Johnny Miller in 1992 he attributed his "mediocre" play in 1989 and his "bad" year in 1990 to his fixation on the mechanics of his swing:

> **That was the first time I felt I was in a slump...I lost the confidence and I was trying to change too many things with the swing and thinking too much of the swing instead of thinking more about score, and that was the problem. (NBC, 1992)**

Later he discussed how children have the natural inclination to "just do it," who don't get caught up in how to do it, yet players constantly search for the secrets to the perfect swing:

If you look at small children, they putt natural, they chip natural, they swing natural, and they never think about anything else besides flipping the ball as soon as possible in the hole—and this is the most important thing—but we [tour pros] all think that there is a secret. And I don't think there is any secret. The only secret is to put the ball as quick as possible into the hole.

Always analyzing, judging, and evaluating your swing hinders you from learning to let it flow.

Many people attribute Fred Couples' success to his ability to play on feel and instinct. He is not concerned with the mechanics of his swing and has not studied his swing in depth like others players have. When he plays he doesn't think about what his clubhead is doing or should be doing on the backswing; instead he pictures the shot he wants and reacts to the environment. Fred Couples talked about trust in an interview during the 1992 Players Championship before going on to win the 1992 Masters. After having two first-place finishes and two second-place finishes early in the season, Couples said:

If I'm on the 18th hole at Riviera, I always think of a good drive I've hit there. I don't think about where the club should be, I just picture the shot and try to hit that shot.

Another misconception is the belief that all bad shots result from a mechanical problem or swing flaw. I would argue that the cause of many poor shots is not mechanical. Bad swings sometimes are initiated mentally by a lapse in concentration, fear, or a lack of confidence. Despite the causes of bad shots, most golfers instantly blame a bad shot on a mechanical flaw without thinking that their alignment was poor or they were not focused on the shot, and analyze their swing and search for a mechanical flaw. PGA player Paul Azinger (1991) wrote:

A lot of amateur players, especially those in the 3 to 8 handi-cap range, are so over-analytical—probably from reading too many instruction articles—that they'll never get any better. Sure you need a key thought, but when they start hitting the ball badly, they get mechanical and start focusing on what they're doing wrong.

The amateur player never considers that a bad shot wasn't due to something other than a mechanical flaw when in fact it might have been caused by the fear of hitting it out-of-bounds or a lapse in con-centration. The mechanical part of the game seems more tangible, and the mental part more abstract. Most golfers falsely assume that there are no "drills" to correct a mental error similar to the drills they have to correct a mechanical flaw.

PROBLEMS WITH TRUSTING YOUR SWING

Lack of trust is another barrier that restricts a golfer from letting it flow. Trust is the ability to hit a shot without interference from your mind. Trust lets you swing the club automatically from memory without thinking about how to swing. Trust is letting go of conscious tendencies to guide the swing through its path. John Daly, after winning the 1991 PGA Championship, said that during the four rounds he didn't think how to swing, he just "hit it."

In fast reactive actions, like hitting a baseball, you do not have enough time to think (it takes less than a .50 seconds for a fastball to travel across the plate), and when the player does think, the ball is past him. If you can hit a successful tee shot with out-of-bounds to the left, water bordering the right side of the fairway, and picture a good shot, but didn't consciously control any part of your swing, then you have experienced trust.

---

*Trust is absolutely
necessary to the feeling
of an effortless swing.*

Without trust, the feeling of an automatic and effortless swing is impossible because, when trust is lacking, the swing requires more conscious energy to execute it.

Chip Beck constantly struggled with being a highly conscious player. In 1989 he almost won the U.S. Open by shooting a course record on the last nine holes, but finished one shot behind. He said that was the first time he was able to let himself play on instinct and not consciously control his shots. He said, "I was just responding, I just let myself go, see the shot and let it go...and that was a big change for me because I had been such a conscious-type player, trying to control and perfect everything."

You can interfere with your ability to trust your swing in many ways. Many barriers to learning to let it flow, such as falling into the practice trap and becoming too focused on perfecting your technique, are long-term problems with trust. But trust ultimately comes down to one decisive moment: when swinging the club.

The Paradox of Control. The first way you interfere with your ability to let it flow is consciously controlling the path of your swing, which is the opposite of trust. There are many reasons why controlling tendencies creep into your swing. A lack of confidence in your ability, fear of hitting a shot into the water, or anxiety can all be the reasons for steering a shot or guiding a putt. Have you ever stood over a putt and just before you began the stroke or during your backswing you told yourself that the putt breaks two more inches to the left than your original judgment indicated, and at the last second manipulated the putter so you could push the ball on your new line? This is an example of consciously controlling your putter to adjust to a split-second change in plans usually caused by an indecision about the correct line.

Fear. A second barrier to trust is fear. Fear of being embarrassed, fear of losing a tournament, and fear of the consequences of a poor shot can ruin a fluid and natural swing. For example, take the fear of not wanting to hit the ball out-of-bounds. You stand on the tee and begin to think how awful it would be if you hit the ball out-of-bounds and then you begin to imagine the ball hooking out-of-bounds. Suddenly you feel yourself getting tense because of the fearful scenario you created in your mind. And bingo! Next, you tried to prevent the ball from traveling out-of-bounds and guided your swing at the last moment to try to hit the ball safely into the fairway. The result was probably a poor shot and the ball hooked out-of-bounds as imagined or missed way right. This happens at all levels of the game. Even Tour pros can lose trust when the heat is on.

Doubt and Indecision. The opposite of doubt and indecision is self-confidence. Doubt can take many forms, the most common of which is doubting your skills or ability to pull off a shot or make a putt. Indecision is also caused by more specific forms of doubt such as doubt about club selection or what line to use when putting. How often have you had a difficult time deciding what club to hit, and at the last split-second before you started to swing, thought, "this is not enough club, so hit it hard." Swinging hard changed your normal rhythm, you lost control over the shot and the ball sailed over the green. The indecision created by being "between clubs" caused you to think that you must control the shot consciously and swing easier or harder.

Indecisive putting also can destroy trust. One big problem for all golfers including PGA Tour professionals is indecision and doubt about what line to select for the putt. After surveying the green and selecting a line, have you ever at the last second changed your mind and played more break than your initial read indicated? Again, the indecision about where to start the putt led to a lack of trust in your stroke, and at the last second you consciously steered the ball off line. The mind was unable to send a clear message to your body about where to hit the putt and consequently the lack of belief in your line created a controlled and awkward stroke.

Anxiety or Worry. A fourth problem that can interfere with your ability to trust is letting anxiety or excessive worry creep into your thoughts. Like fear, anxiety or worry usually leads to excess physical tension. When you become anxious over a five-foot putt that will win the club championship, the anxiety causes your muscles to tighten and change the decision you made about the putt. Trust dwindles as you tighten up and you lose faith in your ability to make the putt, feeling the need to guide the ball on its path rather than make a free stroke. If you leave putts consistently short, you're probably tense or tentative when putting.

Fear of hooking the ball out of bounds causes you to control the swing.

Trying Too Hard. Trying too hard can also destroy trust. The harder you try, the better you play, does not always apply to golf. Trying too hard to steer a putt on line or trying too hard to keep a ball from going into the water can cause you to tense up and hit a tentative shot. Trying hard increases your need to control the swing consciously, which as explained earlier is the opposite of trusting your swing.

Allowing your stroke to flow automatically is particularly important in putting, when precision is at a premium. Guiding your putter through its path by manipulating the putter head ruins your ingrained pattern and obscures the effortless feeling that you have practiced so hard to get. Cindy Figg-Currier says that staying loose on the greens and letting things happen rather than trying too make something happen is very important. She described her attitude for putting during the best performance of her professional career:

> **The less you have to think about the better. When you just loosen up and let your natural ability do what it can do, you can surprise yourself. Instead of trying so hard to make that 40-foot putt go in the hole and really strain and tense up your muscles, then it doesn't happen... I mean you have to be focused on what you're doing, but it's not like you are inching your swing through its path—you just let it happen.**

PERFECTIONISM

A final area that interferes with the development of an automatic and effortless swing is perfectionism. Most perfectionists are extremely goal directed and highly motivated. High motivation is a positive quality in golf when it deals with being dedicated to working hard and practice. High levels of motivation can lead to problems when the need to perfect your swing or technique becomes more important than playing well.

The perfectionist carries this attitude on the golf course. The main goal for the perfectionist is to make flawless swings, rather than getting the ball in the hole. The perfectionist has learned through dedication and a strong work ethic in practice that working hard is more important than playing golf. The perfectionist develops habits without knowing what's happening.

> **You can always find a fault with something, at least with golfers I know or individuals in general. You can always find something that you could have done more perfect.**
> ***Cindy Figg-Currier, LPGA Tour***

I'm amazed when I hear tour pros say they would rather hit the ball well and score poorly during a round than have a good scoring round and hit the ball poorly. For the perfectionist, "playing well" means how solidly they hit the ball, how consistent their technique is, and how good their swing and shot looks. This type of player justifies a poor round by saying: "I didn't score well today but I am hitting the ball well." He or she thinks that scoring occurs later when the mechanics are perfected. Everyone knows that there is no such thing as a perfect swing, so why do golfers keep searching for it? Playing well in golf should translate to how many strokes it takes to play the course, not how good you look in the process.

The perfectionist is more concerned with perfect technique and hard work than playing the game of golf.

You can easily see how a perfectionist attitude can interfere with developing an automated swing. The perfectionist usually focuses solely on mechanics, has problems with trusting the swing, has a fear of failure, and enjoys practicing golf more than playing golf. Thus, the perfectionist maintains all the attitudes that interfere with developing an automatic swing.

ENHANCING AUTOMATICITY AND FLOW

DISCARD SOME BAD HABITS AND ATTITUDES

A good place to start is to shake lose the attitudes and habits of thinking that hinder your ability to develop an automatic swing. You should work on your mechanics and feel confident that your mechanics are sound, but not to the extreme that is counterproductive to developing automaticity. Try to play an entire day without focusing on mechanics or technique. Focus on a general swing key like tempo or rhythm instead of the path of your club. You should have no problem swinging freely if you have ingrained your swing in memory. Experiment with focusing on your target or seeing the shot you want to hit when swinging.

Another ineffective attitude is the idea that you must always be working on your swing to perfect it. The best players in the world will tell you that perfection is impossible in golf. On the PGA Tour, many different functional swings work because each player trusts his or her swing and the results they have produced. Think about the swings of Ray Floyd, Calvin Pete, Lee Trevino, and Miller Barber. They all have uniquely different swings and at times have been criticized for using a method that is not fundamentally sound. Yet, they all have been successful because they believe in their method and trust that they can get good results.

The only thing that is recorded is how many not how you did it.

Believing that you can play well (score well) only after you perfect your technique is an attitude that makes it hard for you to play the game. At some point you have to accept that your mechanics are sound enough to repeat a swing consistently. At times, you need to work on your technique when you have a swing flaw or to improve your swing, but working on technique when playing a round only interferes with your ability to let it flow and play your best golf.

KNOW WHEN TO TRAIN AND WHEN TO PLAY

Knowing when to train and when to free-up your swing helps you to let it flow on the course. At times you need to work on your mechanics. You must train to learn a new move, improve your swing, or correct a swing fault or bad habit. Training is essential for becoming a better golfer. The challenge is to know when to work on mechanics and when to let it rip and just do it. PGA Tour player Tim Simpson has learned how to separate his practice from his play by knowing when to work on mechanics and when to put it on automatic. He said, "I think conscious thoughts when I am working on my game; when I go to the golf course I think flag and hole, flag and hole, and I keep it that simple. As long as I do that I play well."

Earlier I discussed how you must first learn the fundamentals before you can begin to play automatically and effortlessly. To reach this stage it requires a considerable amount of practice. If you make a major swing change, you must replace an old movement pattern with a new one, but this is very difficult to do because you regress back to the acquisition stage of learning. Do you have enough time to make a change before your next tournament or match? You probably would do yourself more harm than good by working on a major swing change close to competition.

The key is to allow yourself enough practice time to ingrain the new move in memory so it can be done on demand, without the old swing popping up occasionally. The problem with playing through a swing change is that your body doesn't know what movement pattern to use because you haven't completely erased the old swing pattern and you haven't totally ingrained a new movement pattern. In competition, your body uses both patterns or a combination of both, which can become confusing. You might consider not making any major mechanical changes in your swing two or more weeks before a match or tournament. One week before a tournament is not enough time to make a major change and still be in a position to let it flow on the course.

If you make a swing change,
allow yourself enough time to
fully ingrain the new movement.

Besides knowing when to train your swing, dedicate part of your time to working on mechanics and part of your practice learning to let it rip and to trust your swing. A misconception about practice is that you always have to be making a change in technique searching for the perfect swing. Not every practice shot has to be focused on the path of your club or the position of your arms at the top or whatever. After fine-tuning your swing, practice trusting it instead of just practicing for practice sake.

INCREASE YOUR TRUST

Trust is an important quality for producing a smooth, rhythmic swing. It is also a requirement for the feeling of an effortless and unconscious swing. Overcontrolling the swing, fear, doubt, indecision, and anxiety all destroy your ability to trust. To increase trust, you must first identify the situations that cause you to lose trust, and then become aware of your tendencies when the heat is on and you don't trust your swing. What typically happens when you lose trust in your swing? Some golfers hold on and don't release the club, others don't transfer their weight and stay back on their rear foot, and still others stab at the ball and stick their club in the ground. Identify your tendencies during practice or competition when you doubted your club selection, became anxious over a difficult shot, or got scared about the possible consequences of a bad shot. Recognizing how you lose trust is the first step in learning to build trust in your swing.

Once you are aware of when you typically lose trust and know what happens when you don't trust, you can work at increasing trust when confronted with similar situations in the future. Take for example, a tee shot with a tight fairway and water bordering the right side. Your lack of trust unconsciously (or consciously) makes you swing less aggressively and stay back on the right foot, causing the ball to hook left. Armed with this information you can deal with the problem head-on. You know the situation and what you typically do in that situation. Consciously decide to make an aggressive swing and use a simple swing key to help you get off your right side. You should try to recognize the fear and then proceed by making an adjustment and overcoming the fear.

REDUCE DOUBT AND INDECISION

Another method for learning to let it flow is to reduce the amount of indecision and doubt you create for yourself. One place to start is to eliminate doubt about your club selection. Whenever you feel you have the wrong club in your hand for the shot, stop and pick a different club. You must believe you have the right club for the shot and swing assertively. Often, you hit a better shot when you swing aggressively and have the wrong club than to swing tentatively with the right club. With the wrong club, you might hit the ball 10 yards too far or too short, with a hesitant swing and right club, you might stick the club in the ground and chunk the ball. The same applies to your decisions about your target and type of shot you want to hit. If you can't be absolute about your decision, make a new decision.

Committing to your read reduces doubt and helps you to hit a shot confidently.

As a rule, you should go with your first instinct and avoid second-guessing yourself.
Tom Kite (1993), PGA Tour

Reducing doubt and indecision is very important in putting. Indecision on the putting green is a major problem for all golfers. Doubting the line you selected for the putt is a sure way to lose trust and hit a tentative putt. It is better to putt decisively with the wrong read, than to putt tentatively having guessed the right line.

How often have you stepped behind the ball, lined up the putt, and found a good line, and then got over the ball and saw a different line and became confused? Why read the putt from behind if you are going to change you mind when you get over the ball? If you read the putt from behind the ball or the other side of the hole, stay committed to your first decision and don't change you mind when you step over the ball. Don't second guess your first instinct, focus on your line as you approach the ball—don't lose sight of it. Commit to your line! Chapter 7 discusses other ways of increasing trust by using your preshot routine.

TRY LESS

Trying too hard can destroy trust. The harder you try, the more you consciously control your swing. Controlling your swing is the opposite of trust. Sometimes trying less is better. Bob Tway explains that trying less requires you to have a detached attitude:

> **There is a fine line between trying too hard and not trying too hard. I don't know the answer to that, it's a tough deal. You need to play golf like you don't care, but if you work at something your whole life, how do you not care? But that is the way you need to play golf, you need to sit on the first tee and not care, just let the ball go, that's how you play your greatest golf.**

Trying less doesn't mean giving up or concentrating less. Trying less means not grinding over every shot and mechanically making your swing happen. Trying less means letting what you have practiced come to the surface and relying on you body to execute.

PRACTICE FOR TRUST AND AUTOMATICITY

As discussed earlier, sometimes you must work on your mechanics, and other times you need to stop analyzing and just look at the target and let it rip. The next step is to learn how to free up your mind in practice to help you get into the trusting frame of mind. You must *learn* to trust your swing in practice. This is a time to shut off your active, analytical mind and allow yourself to hit the shot automatically from memory. When you practice to improve mechanics, the conscious mind is in control. When you practice for automaticity and trust, conscious instructions are kept to a minimum. In a sense, you are allowing yourself to hit the shot from a memory pattern that you have grooved over thousands and thousands of swings. You must quiet your mind by not taking conscious control of your swing.

Some people find this difficult because they don't feel as though they are trying hard enough. Not trying to do something consciously with the swing seems aimless to some people. Yet with this free state of mind the swing is pure and undiluted. Try experimenting in practice to free-up yourself. One exercise you can use to free yourself up is to practice swinging or hitting balls with your eyes closed and observing how your swing feels. You can't steer the ball to the target if you cannot see the target directly or through your peripheral vision. Switch off between eyes closed and eyes open until you can feel the same results with your eyes open.

Another method to free your mind is to find a swing key that allows you to focus on the rhythm, tempo, or pace of your swing. Instead of giving yourself mechanical instructions during the swing, focus on a general swing key like the cadence of your swing on the backswing and downswing. This gets your mind off the details of a correct swing while allowing you to focus on a very important aspect of the swing and free yourself to hit the shot from memory. Tim Gallwey (1979) in *The Inner Game of Golf* recommends that you say to yourself the word "back" on the backswing and "hit" on the downswing to quiet your analytical mind, just another way of improving trust and letting yourself hit the shot.

*Find a swing key that helps
you to swing effortlessly.*

What happens when you trust your swing and hook three tee shots in a row? Total trust is hard to identify for some golfers. You may feel they you were on automatic pilot but really were not. What should you do? Is it time to abandon trust and go back to mechanically guiding the swing to get the ball in the fairway? No, most likely the results get worse. A better alternative is to let it flow and work on a swing key after the round or another more suitable time. At least you have a shot pattern you can work with and anticipate. The other option is to tamper with the swing, confuse yourself more, and then not know where your next shot will go.

If you totally trusted your swing and the shot was poor, then it may be time to make some changes in the swing, but not on the golf course! When playing, you must play with what you have—you don't have enough time to make changes or modify your swing. If you have some type of pattern to your shots, you at least can anticipate what the ball does. Anticipate and play the shot that you are hitting until you have time to make the appropriate changes.

GO WITH THE FLOW

Start disciplining yourself to trust your swing in practice if you have problems with trust on the course. Practice does not pay off unless you can take your game to the course. Commit yourself to letting the swing flow automatically. A preswing cue to focus you in on letting it flow should be a part of your preshot routine. Integrating a preswing thought into your routine like "let it rip," "let it go," or "free it up" are good cues. Go with the flow, you may surprise yourself.

CHAPTER SUMMARY

• Getting caught in the practice trap, overanalyzing the technical part of the game, lack of trust, and perfectionistic tendencies hurt your ability to let it flow.

• You must discard the attitudes that inhibit you from learning to let it flow, such as thinking you always have to work on mechanics when you practice.

• Know when to work on your swing and when to let it rip. You must decide when to work on technique and then give enough time to reach automatic execution before you compete.

• Increase you trust by knowing when you lose faith in your swing and have a preplanned strategy to help you let it flow.

• Devote part of your practice to learning to swing freely without focusing on how to swing.

IMMERSE YOURSELF
IN THE SHOT

I began to acquire my powers of concentration long ago when learning to create a variety of shots with only my old 3-iron. I had to focus very intensely indeed on the grip, the setup, and the swing path to get the results I wanted out of that awkward, overlong club, and it taught me how to enter a mental cocoon, which today insures that every shot I play gets my undivided attention.
Seve Ballesteros (1988)

The ability to concentrate in the present and on the task at hand is very important to achieve peak performance in any sport. During an average four-hour round, usually only about 30 minutes are spent focusing attention on execution of shots. Switching concentration on and off makes it especially difficult to get into the flow. Total concentration occurs when you become totally involved in the task, you feel like time is suspended, and you lose the sense of being separate from your surroundings.

Total concentration occurs when you focus in the present on each shot, become immersed in the relevant stimuli to hit the shot, and don't allow yourself to be detached from the task at hand. Golfers who report being totally immersed describe it as a blending of action and awareness. The mind focuses so intensely on the task at hand that it's difficult to separate the self from the task. For a brief moment, the mind becomes lost in the experience of getting the ball from point A to point B. The psychological self seems inseparable from the physical process and demands of the shot.

Concentration also is the ability to refocus your attention when distracted. It is sometimes easy to be distracted by external disruptions such as other players talking or by your inner dialogue during a round of golf. You must learn to recognize when you're not focused on the shot and refocus your attention on task-relevant stimuli.

Some golfers choose to focus for the entire time they are on the golf course, which places even greater demands on concentration. Ben Hogan was this type of player. He preferred to concentrate on his game for the entire round. Whereas, someone like Lee Trevino prefers to focus only when it is his turn to hit. Whatever style you prefer, to hit your best shot requires you to focus intensely on each shot when it is your turn to play.

Concentration is important when coping with the adverse effects of anxiety. As tension begins to mount, focusing intensely on the task at hand is a great method for riding yourself or tuning out anxiety provoking thoughts. Jack Nicklaus focuses more forcefully on his shots when he feels the pressure mount, stating that concentration is "focusing the mind so firmly and so positively on the job at hand as to squeeze out all superfluous and negative thoughts." (Nicklaus & Bowden, 1974)

WHAT DO YOU FOCUS ON?

Most golfers generally know what concentration is and how to concentrate but not what they should concentrate on. Concentration is selectively focusing on the task relevant cues in your game and not allowing yourself to become distracted by internal or external disturbances. David Edwards described concentration the following way:

My mental energy is consummed with whatever it is that I'm trying to accomplish. It's like tunnel vision versus peripheral vision. The only thing that I'm really seeing or thinking about is the shot or whatever, versus somebody walking by or whatever else is going on like what I'm going to do the next day or what time the flight leaves.

Focusing your attention on one shot at a time requires that you know what cues to focus on and when to focus, and to have an awareness of when you are not focusing.

Concentration not only involves focusing your mind but it also includes focusing on the cues that facilitate performance.

To fully concentrate, you must know the requirements of each shot and the type of focus that facilitates performance. Concentration by itself will not help you play better unless you are concentrating on the features that are important to your performance. Most amateur golfers don't know what features of shot preparation they should focus on to hit their best shot.

YOUR ATTENTION VARIES DURING SHOT PREPARATION

Your focus varies during the preparation and execution of each shot. To prepare for a shot or a putt you must consider many factors, including the demands of the shot and the environmental and course conditions. Generally, your attention goes through three different phases: (1) analyzing the situation and planning the shot; (2) preparing and programming for the shot; and (3) executing the shot.

You have to assess several factors when analyzing the requirements of an approach shot including the environmental conditions (wind, rain, temperature), the lie of the ball, the distance to the target, the landing area, trouble areas of the shot, and so on. You then select a club based on this information. Next, you prepare your mind and body for the shot based on your assessment of the situation and how you planned the shot. Your preparation for the shot might include imagining the ball flying to the target, feeling the correct shot while taking a practice swing, setting up and aligning to a target, and waggling the club and glancing at the target. In the final stage, you fixate your attention on executing the shot and getting the ball to the target. The second before you begin the backswing until after the ball is struck is the critical time for the performance of the shot. You might focus on the target and become absorbed with the image of the shot or use a swing key for tempo or rhythm during this time.

When you assess the requirements of a putt, you must consider the slope of the green, the speed and grain of the green, the distance to the target, the influence of any wind, et cetera, and decide on the correct line and speed to hit the putt. As you prepare for a putt, you might imagine the ball rolling along your intended line, feel the distance of the stroke with a practice swing, set up and align to your target, and glance a couple of times at the target. Finally, you direct your attention to executing the putt and getting the ball to roll along your line. You focus on your line and become absorbed in the putt rolling along your line into the hole. You might feel the distance or tempo of the swing during this time. Thus, your attention varies as you plan, prepare, and execute each shot or putt. If you focus exclusively on the right elements, you increase your chances to get into the flow and hit your best shot.

To concentrate on one shot at a time, you must know more than just what to focus on. You must also recognize when you are not focused on the cues that facilitate performance and be able to refocus your attention back to those ingredients. The challenge is to keep focused on the elements of shot preparation and refocus your attention on those element when under pressure or when you're bombarded by distractions.

---

*You must know more than just
what to focus on. You also
must recognize when you're not
focused and be able to refocus.*

Are You Involved?

Many attentional problems stem from the inability to recognize when you are distracted and not focused properly on the shot. You must learn to recognize when you are distracted, like when you start to think about the party you're going to that night. Your attention becomes disconnected by several pieces of information that compete for your attention and pulls you off task. Your attention can become detached by either external distractions (i.e., playing partners talking or moving) or internal distractions (i.e., thoughts unrelated to the shot). Both internal and external distractions are equally damaging to your performance. The following section describes some typical ways that attention wanders from the task at hand.

OUTER ANNOYANCES AND INNER DISTURBANCES

Most players' attention wanders back and forth from one thought to the next. To stay focused on one thought or object for an extended period of time is extremely difficult for anyone to do. Fortunately, you only have to focus for a maximum of 30 to 40 seconds at one time to prepare for and execute a shot. Yet, you have many opportunities for your mind to drift during that period. Anything in your environment can be potentially distracting. Playing partners, conditions of the course, weather conditions, and noise can all pull your attention away from the shot.

Do you have a tough time focusing when your playing partners are talking in the background or walking around when you are hitting? If you think about poor weather (wind or rain) or poor course conditions (bumpy greens), you can become diverted from your task. Many players, including professionals, become distracted when they hear the smallest sound in the background.

> **The most important thing I can do is stay in the present, but you got to remember that's the hardest thing to do. It's easy to think about what's going to happen tomorrow or what happened yesterday. The hardest thing to do is stay in control today.**
> *Kelly Gibson, PGA Tour*

External distractions are trivial compared to the self-inflicted internal dialogue that tugs your thoughts away from the task at hand.

It's easier said than done, but you must learn to focus your mind in the present if you are to hit your best shot and play to your potential. Do you distract yourself by thinking about what happened on the last hole or your drive the following hole? Standing over a shot thinking about the last putt you missed or the last shot you sliced into the water won't help you hit the shot your trying to play. Thinking about the next tee shot on the 15th hole while trying to sink your putt on the 14th hole only diverts your attention from the putt you are trying to make.

FINDING YOUR ZONE

You probably have discovered that you can concentrate better when there is something on the line or when you are excited about playing golf. Also, you might have observed that your concentration is poor when the situation is not challenging enough for you or for whatever reason you're just not excited about playing. Similarly, most likely you have experienced times when your concentration was poor when you were too anxious, tense, or keyed up to play your best.

Everyone has an ideal zone of excitement for optimal performance. When you are either too excited (or under extreme pressure) or you are too bored (lack of challenge), your performance suffers. As you become more "up" and excited to play, the better your concentration becomes, up to a point where you become too aroused and the challenge is too great for you. For example, Jack Nicklaus (1974) said his concentration improves when he becomes excited and challenged by the situation:

> **Whenever I am "up" for golf—when either the tournament or the course, or best of all, both, excite and challenge me—I have little trouble concentrating, and therefore little trouble with tension. But whenever the occasion doesn't challenge me, or I am simply jaded with golf, then it is time I have to bear down on myself with a vengeance.**

When you are under intense pressure and become too excited, you stop focusing on important cues and focus more on the thoughts that are producing anxiety, such as thinking about missing a putt for par. Thus, there is an optimal zone for your concentration that is influenced by your level of excitement or anxiety and your perception of the challenge of the situation. Chapter 6 discusses how to maintain an optimal level of arousal. The rest of this chapter provides methods of helping you to focus on the shot at hand, eliminate unwanted distractions and find your zone.

CONCENTRATE ON ONE SHOT AT A TIME

To play your best, it is critical to focus your complete attention on each and every shot. If you are a fast player, it takes about 20 seconds to prepare for a shot; if you are slow you may spend 30 to 40 seconds preparing for a shot. In that period, you need to be totally engrossed into cues that help you to hit your best shot. Thinking about the last putt you missed reduces the energy available for the present shot. Likewise, getting ahead of yourself by thinking about a possible finishing score for the day has the same effect.

The biggest error made by amateur golfers is that they don't focus in the present on the immediate shot.

You get ahead of yourself by thinking about winning, a finishing score, or the consequences of missing a par putt. When you think about results, you only induce more pressure and create greater tension. As tension increases, you start to focus more on outcomes and then become even more tense and fearful.

You must have a presence of mind to know when you are not focusing on the elements of shot preparation and execution. Once you recognize when your mind is wandering, you can learn to refocus on the present shot and on what you need to think about to hit your best shot.

67

DEVELOP A PRESHOT ROUTINE

The preshot routine is an excellent tool to help you prepare for and focus on each shot, and refocus your attention when distracted. The preshot routine is a blending of preparatory actions that help you analyze, prepare, and execute each shot. The preshot routine combines physical actions (practice swing, waggles, and looks at the target) and specific thoughts or images (visualizing the flight of the ball, focusing on the target, and using a swing key) to keep you focused in the present for each shot. The specific ingredients of a preshot routine vary from person to person, depending on each person's unique idiosyncrasies. Chapter 7 introduces preshot routines and discusses the elements of a routine in more detail.

It is easier to focus on each shot when you have a set routine and know exactly when and where to divert your attention. The routine diverts your attention on the ingredients of shot preparation that facilitate performance. Jack Nicklaus said, "the busier you can keep yourself with the particulars of shot assessment and execution, the less chance your mind has to dwell on the emotional 'if' and 'but' factors that breed anxiety." (Ferguson, 1972) A routine also assists you by helping you to recognize when you're not giving full attention to the shot. A set routine helps you prepare the same way on each shot and each putt. When you're not absorbed in the elements of your routine, it is an indication that your drifting to irrelevant cues.

When you have a set routine, you will find it easier to notice when you're distracted and not within the boundary of your normal routine. It is important to recognize when you are not in the flow of your normal shot preparation. When this happens, you need to stop yourself, refocus on your routine, and begin the routine over. If you could refocus your mind for just five shots during a round, wouldn't that make a difference in your performance? The routine must flow from start to finish just like a good swing. When you notice that you are distracted and your normal routine is interrupted, refocus and get immersed in the components of your routine.

A preshot routine focuses you on the essential ingredients of shot preparation and helps you detect when your not focused properly.

DON'T TRY TO BLOCK OUT DISTRACTIONS

Most golfers assume that you must consciously eliminate distractions, but this is the wrong approach. Instead, you need to refocus on the task rather than block out the distraction. For example, when you try to block out a noise while you are putting, it only makes you focus more on the distracting noise. Trying to block out a distraction is similar to telling yourself not to hit the ball in the

The more you think about the water, the more in focus the water becomes.

water. You only focus more on the water and this causes you to try to avoid it. Obviously it would be better to focus on the center of the fairway, not the water.

You cannot eliminate distractions by trying not to think about them. This only brings the distraction more clearly into your awareness. Rather, shift your focus back to what you need to do to hit a good shot, which requires you to focus intensely on the components of your shot preparation. When you shift your attention back and become immersed in the ingredients of your routine, the distractions becomes secondary. If you can totally immerse yourself in the shot, you lose your awareness of the distraction.

> **You don't want to think about eliminating distractions. If you think more about what you want to do rather than what you don't want to do, you're a lot better off.**
> *D.A. Weibring, PGA Tour*

The idea of refocusing your attention is similar to shifting your vision back and forth from two objects at different distances. When you look at an object that is 50 feet away, you lose sight of objects that are right in front of you. When you focus on an object that is right in front of you, objects in the distance disappear and fall into the background of your vision until you shift your vision back.

Refocusing your attention works the same way. When your attention drifts during putting because you became aware of something in the "background" (someone talking), refocus on the ingredients of your routine so that the distraction drops out of focus and blends into the background. Don't block out the distraction, focus intensely on your preparation for the shot. Seve Ballesteros is a model of intense concentration when he plays. He focuses his attention on each shot by creating an imaginary tunnel to his target and then immersing himself in his setup and the rest of his routine. He focuses so intensely on what he is trying to accomplish that distractions are not a problem when he plays:

> **By the time the tournament arrives, I'm so deeply immersed in my game plan and my play that I'm virtually oblivious to outside sights and sounds. For instance, I never hear my playing partner's clubs rattling, and I rarely ever hear the gallery applauding. Even after a round, when I return to my hotel room, all hell could break loose and I would never know it. I'm in a world of my own. (Ballesteros, 1988)**

An effective drill that I use to teach players to focus intensely on the task is to distract them purposely in practice when they are hitting shots or putting. I'll ask them to focus intensely on their preparation for the shot rather than focus on the obnoxious noise that I am making. If the player laughs, I know he has trouble doing the drill. The player soon learns to get so involved in hitting the shot that distractions blend into the background.

You must learn to recognize when you are distracted and refocus your attention on the task at hand. This is why a preshot routine is so important. You know exactly what you should be focused on if you have a set routine to follow. Recognizing when you're not concentrating requires that you first know the appropriate attentional elements to focus on. If you're not focused on hitting a good shot, begin your routine over from the start so your preparation flows into the swing.

FOCUS ON WHAT YOU WANT TO HAPPEN, NOT WHAT YOU FEAR MIGHT HAPPEN

A big challenge for all golfers is focusing on what they want to happen rather than getting caught up in what they fear might happen. Golf courses designers construct courses to intimidate golfers with trouble areas that are positioned strategically on each hole. Out-of-bounds, water hazards, ponds, trees, fairway bunkers, and fairway traps are the trouble regions that can cause you to doubt yourself.

These areas on the golf course don't cause you to fear a shot unless you let them. The water hazard doesn't trigger you to fear a tee shot unless you allow yourself to fear the water hazard by focusing more on avoiding it than on the shot you want to hit. You must learn to break the habit of focusing on the trouble or thinking about making a mistake.

> **If you start seeing mistakes or trouble, it's like a habit, you keep doing it—you set yourself up to do the same thing the next time.**
> *Trevor Dodds, PGA Tour*

Take the example of a tee shot with water down the right side of the fairway. You stand on the tee and it's your turn to hit. You think to yourself, "Don't hit it in the water." You become absorbed in avoiding the water. The thought creates an image in your mind of the ball slicing into the water and the emotional reaction that follows. By thinking about not hitting the ball into the water, you have already hit the ball into the water in your mind! Your body doesn't understand the meaning of the word no, or the difference between a positive and a negative command. Your physical self interprets "don't hit it into the water" as meaning "hit it into the water" because you have programmed your physical self to do just that.

You also destroy your ability to trust your swing in this situation (refer to Chapter 4). As you consciously try not to hit the ball into the water, you change the tempo and rhythm of your swing. Most likely, when you steer the ball away from the water, you overcompensate and hit the ball too far away from the water or you hit it in the water.

You obviously would prefer to play "smart golf" and strategically place your shots to allow for some margin of error. To play smart, you at least have to acknowledge the trouble and develop a strategy for hitting the shot. The problem arises when your mind becomes too involved in thinking about the trouble instead of what you want to have happen with the shot. Once you decide where you want to hit the shot based on the areas you want to avoid, then it is necessary to keep your mind focused on what you want to do with the shot. Think about where you want to land the shot, or you might want to picture in your mind the type of shot you want to hit—if you are going to hit a fade or a draw, high or low shot. Your challenge is to involve yourself in what you want to do with the shot after you made your decision on where to hit it.

Direct Your Attention To What You Can Control

Controlling your attention means understanding what things are in your control during a round. You unnecessarily distract yourself if you become occupied with things over which you have no direct control. What things can you control? You can control your thoughts, feelings, and emotions when playing. You have control over the way you mentally and physically prepare for shots and putts. You can control how you react to missing a short putt. You may not be able to completely control making a five-foot putt for par, but you do have control over how you react to missing the five foot putt for par.

What can't you control? Many factors influence the outcome of any shot or putt that are beyond your direct control. You can only influence the ball before making contact, after impact whatever happens is beyond your control. You cannot control the natural elements, such as a sudden gust of wind, chance factors like your ball bouncing in the wrong direction, or poor conditions of the course, such as imperfections in the green. Amateur golfers ask me how to deal with frustration, such as when a ball comes to rest in a divot. The answer is simple. A ball that stops in a divot is bad luck and nothing else. You had no influence over the ball coming to rest in a divot so why get upset over something that was just bad luck?

Getting upset will only hurt you on the next shot because of increased tension. You must learn to accept whatever the course and environment gives you. After the ball leaves the clubface there is a lot of luck in the outcome of any shot or putt.

Take putting for example. You have no influence over the roll of the ball after your putter makes contact with the ball. Spike marks, foot prints, imperfections in the grass, unexpected variations in the grain, and wind and moisture can cause you to miss a perfectly hit putt. Don't concern yourself or become upset with the things that you have no power over—they are a natural part of the game.

*Don't concern yourself with
bad breaks, course conditions, or
what your opponents are doing
because all are beyond your control.*

You also can't control the performance of your opponents. This is irrelevant to your play and you shouldn't concern yourself with what they are doing. You lose energy by thinking about what your opponent is doing, and you allow yourself to be distracted from your real purpose. You shouldn't think about winning the match because that is irrelevant to your immediate goal. The outcome of a match is decided by more that just how well you play. Focus on playing the course to the best of your ability instead of thinking about what your opponent does.

To think like the pros you need to focus on doing the best you can on each shot. Performing your best on each shot requires you to focus on the factors that allow you to hit your best shot. Focusing on things beyond your control only detracts from that purpose. Mentally and physically preparing yourself for each shot to the best of your ability by being focused, confident, and trusting on each shot will allow you to play the best you can.

ENGAGE WITH THE TARGET

What you focus on when executing a shot is critical to optimal performance. You are either focused externally on a target or internally on thoughts or images. When preparing to hit a shot, your attention shifts back and forth from an internal to an external focus, depending on the requirements of the shot and the stage of your preparation. Typically, when preparing for a shot, you assess the situation (external), select a club based on past outcomes (internal), image or feel the shot you want to hit (internal), set up and align to a target (external), focus on a swing key (internal), and engage with the target (external). Your attention shifts back and forth from internal to external, depending on the specific stage of shot preparation,

75

but eventually your attention shifts externally to your target. Tim Simpson described his focus when he won the 1989 USF&G Classic in New Orleans. He said the last round of the tournament was the best performance of his career because he was able to control his focus even with the pressure of leading a tournament, and thus played to his potential:

> **I focused so hard on the target that I know my body will do what my mind is telling it to do. Which is telling it nothing other than "that's where I want you to hit it—now you do it," with your God-given talent and your thousands of hours of practice over the years.**

Shifting your attention from internal, mechanical cues to your target when you are ready to pull the trigger helps you become target-oriented. An internal focus helps you to analyze the situation and select a course of action, but sometimes it's difficult to pull away from an internal focus. Problems occur when you can't break away from the analyzing, judging, and evaluating that occurs when focused internally. Golfers who think too much about mechanics at address get locked into an internal focus.

Learn to become target-oriented by directing your attention to the target or putting line as you prepare to execute your shot. This allows you to respond automatically to the cues in the environment, which facilitates automatic execution of the swing (refer to Chapter 4 on letting it flow). You become locked into an internal focus when you are overly concerned with mechanics, consume yourself with the outcome of a shot, or worry whether you selected the correct club. Getting into the flow and responding to the target occurs when you assess the situation, prepare for the shot, and allow yourself to react externally to your target.

CHAPTER SUMMARY

• To concentrate effectively you must know what cues to focus on, recognize when you are not focused on those cues, and refocus your attention when needed.

• You need to find your zone for optimal concentration. If you become either too aroused or you are too bored, your performance suffers. When you become too aroused, learn to relax. When you are bored, create a challenge to increase your involvement.

• Play one shot at a time. If you start to think ahead about the holes to come, refocus your attention on the shot that you are presently playing.

• Develop a preshot routine so when you become distracted, you know on what to refocus your attention.

• Trying to block out a distraction only brings it clearer into focus. Focus intensely on what you are trying to do with the shot rather than paying attention to the distraction.

• Discipline yourself to focus on what you want to happen rather than focusing on what you want to avoid doing.

• You should be concerned with only the things that you can control. Don't become frustrated over events over which you have no control.

• Direct your attention externally and focus on responding to your target when preparing to execute a shot.

6

CONTROLLING YOUR EMOTIONS

I try to make pressure and tension work for me. I want the adrenaline to be flowing. I think sometimes we try so hard to be cool, calm, and collected that we forget what we are doing. There's nothing wrong with being charged up if it's controlled.
Hale Irwin (Ferguson, 1972)

Intense pressure, excess muscular tension, and lack of emotional control can be harmful to any athlete's performance. Learning how to control your emotions and not letting your emotions rule you is a key to playing in the zone. A player who manages his emotions has an advantage over the player who plays out of control.

Playing in the zone creates a mixture of positive emotions, and these emotions are helpful to attaining peak performance. Feeling energized but calm, pumped-up but in control, and intense but relaxed are emotions that are conducive to peak performance. Positive emotions and emotional control are typical of playing in the zone, but you don't always play in the zone, and it's necessary to work at controlling your emotions to win the inner battle.

Players of all levels experience pressure and anxiety, but it's how a player deals with pressure that separates the champion from the choker. The anxiety that a tour pro endures from the pressure to make birdie on the last hole to win the U.S. Open is similar to the anxiety the amateur golfer feels from needing to sink a five-foot putt for par to win a one-dollar wager. Paul Azinger said, "I've never been so nervous before as I was today," after winning the 1992 Tour Championship. Yet he managed to win the battle within and win the event. The source of pressure for the tour pro and amateur player is very different, but the uncomfortable feelings that accompany anxiety are very similar.

Pressure is what you make of it. Pressure starts on the outside and can lead to anxiety and uneasiness, or a feeling of excitement and thrill. Playing in a club championship or putting to win a match are external pressures that potentially can induce anxiety or instill excitement. If the pressure to sink a putt on the last hole to win a match makes you anxious, you feel apprehensive, uneasy, worried, or scared, and ruin you chance of making the putt. If the pressure to make the putt on the last hole intensifies your concentration, your chance of making the putt improve. The goal of this chapter is to help you control your emotions and find your optimal zone of functioning.

USING PRESSURE TO YOUR ADVANTAGE

Pressure is not always harmful to your performance. Pressure increases your motivation to practice, boosts your concentration to help you hit a difficult shot, and supplies extra energy or adrenaline for a long drive. Pressure becomes a problem only when you don't cope with it and it takes you out of your optimal emotional zone.

Excitement and increased arousal helps you to play better, except when it reaches a point where you become overaroused, and then your play worsens. A difficult shot that challenges you beyond your capabilities may cause you to worry, tighten up, chop at the ball and chunk the shot. On the other hand, your performance also suffers when you're not intense enough because you lack concentration and energy to hit the shot.

Pressure can help or
hurt, depending
on how you use it.

79

Pressure, if not handled properly, can trigger internal fears, which lead to overarousal. When overaroused, your muscles tighten, causing you to swing fast or jerky. Muscular tension also destroys the most mechanically sound putting stroke. When tense, your muscles fight each other to a deadlock. You grip the club too tightly, jerk the club down from the top of the swing, flinch on the downswing, or fail to release the club through impact. The negative effects of muscular tension can be very subtle, especially with putting where precision is at a premium. Small increases in muscular tension are often imperceptible, but they can ruin a smooth putting stroke.

The psychological effects of pressure are also harmful if not controlled. Anxiety spoils your normal pace, causing you to speed up most of your behaviors. When anxious, you walk faster, swing quicker and harder, and lose tempo and rhythm. Anxiety also increases doubt and indecision, which hurts your confidence. Anxiety narrows your visual field, causing you to make poor decisions because of the loss of information needed to plan for a shot.

How Much is Too Much?

Everyone has a different zone of optimal arousal, when if exceeded, anxiety or overarousal ensues. Some players play better when they are relaxed, others play better at high levels of intensity. The perception of excitement is a positive state of readiness, whereas anxiety is a negative state of overarousal. As excitement and arousal increase, concentration and energy increase. Cindy Figg-Currier explained how she plays her best when she is excited but in control of herself:

> **I think a good kind of anxious helps. You're excited, but it is very controlled. You have control over your emotions, your emotions don't have control over you... You use that energy when you're excited to help you hit it closer to the hole and get that nice big drive down the fairway, instead of the excitement making you nervous and pulling your drive.**

The key is to find your zone and know when you exceed your threshold. Many amateurs are unable to recognize when they are anxious or rigid. You can't confront what you can't see. Learning to recognize when you get out of your zone is the first step to controlling your emotions. The sooner you recognize overarousal, the quicker you can take control before it gets out of hand.

One way to tune into your optimal zone is to contrast your best and worst performances. Can you identify with the feelings and emotions when you were playing well compared to when you were playing poorly? How relaxed or tight were you? How much pressure did you perceive? Did you feel excited about playing? Assessing your past performances is a good way to find your optimal zone.

In golf, you try to keep on an even keel, don't get too excited, don't get too down, if possible.
Bob Tway, PGA Tour

IDENTIFYING YOUR REACTIONS

Pressure is not harmful unless you interpret it as such. Trying to win a club championship is potentially stressful but you don't become anxious until you think you are threatened. If you feel too challenged by a club championship, you become anxious. Each person responds differently to playing in a club championship because of how a person interprets an event. Anxiety occurs when you think the challenge is beyond your skill level and ability to cope. Later, I discuss how to make the pressure work for you instead of against you.

LEARN TO IDENTIFY WHEN YOU ARE STRESSED

The best way to deal with pressure is to not allow your mind to be filled with anxiety producing thoughts, and to cut them short before they lead to anxiety. This may not be easy for some players. If you do become anxious, you must have a strategy to counter its negative effects. The first step in controlling your emotions is to learn to recognize the signs of overarousal and tension. Then you can develop strategies to respond to pressure in a positive way, eliminating the negative effects of anxiety.

Taking control begins by recognizing the situations that stress you, and then understanding how you personally react in those situations. What specific pressure situations cause you to feel scared, tentative, anxious, or tense? Does your play get worse in pressure situations? Do you try too hard when you are trying to impress someone with whom you are playing? Do difficult shots cause you to think about negative results and cause you to tighten up and swing faster?

The next step is learning to recognize the signs and symptoms of anxiety and overarousal. When you get in a pressure situation, what happens to you physically and mentally? What happens to your performance in that situation? Use Table 1 to identify your typical physical, mental, and behavioral responses when anxious.

TABLE 1
Physical, Mental, and Behavioral Responses to Stress

Physical	Mental	Behavioral
• Rapid heart rate	• Worry	• Walk faster
• Increased respiration	• Feeling confused	• Swing faster
• Increased blood pressure	• Poor concentration	• Jabby putting stroke
• Increased muscle tension	• Feeling not in control	• "Death grip"
• Butterflies in stomach	• Attention narrows	• Poor release of club
• Increased sweating	• Forgetfulness	• Poor read of green
• Dry mouth	• Mental errors	• Pacing
• Frequent urination		• Nail biting
• Increased adrenalin		
• Trembling		

The goal is to learn to recognize overarousal sooner so as to get back into your zone. The quicker you can recognize signs of stress, the faster you can control it before it gets beyond control. Later, I discuss how to take control of your physical state of activation.

THINK LIKE A CHAMPION

To think like the pros, you must develop mental skills to deal with adversity. You must learn to think about pressure as a friend rather than an enemy. Pressure can be helpful or a handicap. It can increase your energy and improve your concentration, or if you let the pressure get to you, you become anxious and worry about failing. How you think under tournament pressure is up to you.

> **I'm a big believer in that's what you work for. If you don't like the pressure when you get there, you're wasting your time... I take the attitude "I've worked hard to get here and have a chance to win—lets go for it."**
> *D.A. Weibring, PGA Tour*

IT ISN'T ALL BAD

Your response to stress is a natural reaction to heightened levels of perceived pressure. The stress response, also called the "fight or flight" response, occurs when you think you're in physical danger or psychologically threatened. Heightened arousal is a functional response that helped our ancestors prepare to fight or flee from physical danger. When you feel fear about missing a short putt to win a match, the increase in adrenaline, heart rate, blood pressure, and respiration function to prepare your body and mind for action to deal with threat. Since you are never in physical danger when you play golf, the anxiety you experience is triggered by a perception of threat to your self-esteem or ego.

The increased adrenaline you experience when trying to avoid a car accident is very helpful to your safety. When you get scared over making a five-foot putt for par, excess tension only ruins a fluid stroke. The worry, fear, and tentativeness you feel about missing a putt is not an abnormal reaction in that situation, but if you don't learn to control your emotions in that situation, anxiety gets the best of you. Everyone has similar feelings when under stress, but what separates a person who chokes from the person who copes is how he deals with those feelings. The choker tunes into the uncomfortable feelings, becomes more apprehensive, and lets anxiety intensify. The person who copes with the situation learns to use the pressure to help focus more intensely on the task.

---

*There is a fine line
between choking and
coping with pressure.*

Many golfers think that something is wrong with them when they freeze over putts and can't pull the putter back. Players are relieved when they discover that they're not the only one who struggles with the same uncomfortable feelings. Even tour pros struggle, especially when they're leading a tournament and playing the last nine holes with a one-shot lead. Many tour pros enjoy the challenge of handling their emotions when they are in contention to win a tournament. Winning the inner battle is what it's all about for them. When you learn to interpret pressure as useful to focusing on the task and heightening your energy, your chances of playing in the zone improve.

WHERE'S YOUR FOCUS?

When you think about hitting a tee shot out-of-bounds, focus on missing a short putt for par, worry about embarrassing yourself or failing, you are sure to get anxious. Anxiety and fear usually are produced by thinking about the results of your actions. Your fear is directed toward future outcomes: "What if I fail and lose the match?" When you focus on negative results, your anxiety increases, causing you to play poorly.

A key to staying in control is to maintain your focus in the present on the process of performing. You're not focused on making the putt when you get ahead of yourself and think about missing the five-foot putt for par. You have the option of either focusing on making the putt or thinking about how awful it would be if you missed the putt. Nick Faldo believes that a good way to battle pressure is to focus on the task. He focuses so intensely on his preshot routine or a swing cue that there is no room for negative thoughts to enter his mind.

Learn to focus your mind on the here and now—on the process of your immediate task. Think about your preshot routine or a swing cue that allows you to hit a good shot. When you catch yourself thinking about results, refocus back to the process of shot preparation. This requires that you recognize when you're not focused on the shot, release any negative thoughts, and refocus on your preparation. Use the three-R method: recognize, release, and refocus.

You're not focused on the task at hand when thinking ahead about negative results.

DO YOU HAVE PRIORITIES?

The more important it is to play well, the more anxiety you experience when under pressure. As players rise to higher levels of competition, the importance of playing well increases. Young professionals who attempt to qualify for the PGA Tour during Tour

Qualifying School, play under a great amount of pressure. It is a high priority for young professionals, because it determines their playing status for the next year or maybe for the next few years. A weekend amateur golfer, although not playing to join the tour, places almost as much importance on playing well in a weekend round with friends.

The more you have to win or play well, the more pressure you put on yourself, which increases anxiety. Even professionals need to keep a good perspective on golf. Golf is a big part of a tour pro's life, but it's not their entire life. They still have their family, friends, other business pursuits, and hobbies. If they lose a tournament or play poorly, they know their family still loves them for who they are, not what they can do. It's not like they won't get another chance the next day when the sun comes up.

It's a mistake to tie your feeling of self-worth to how well you perform on a given day. If you play poorly, can you still be happy with yourself? Measuring your self-worth by how well you play generates higher levels of anxiety and makes you try even harder to play well. You need to separate your performance in golf from you as a person. Your athletic personality is just one aspect of your total being.

WHAT IS THE WORST THAT CAN HAPPEN?

Many golfers place undue pressure on themselves by thinking ahead about all the terrible things that might happen if they mess up a shot. For example, thinking how awful it would be if you missed a crucial approach shot only causes you to freeze up and cripple yourself with negative thinking. Making a short putt becomes a life or death contest when you overstate the significance of missing. This is called catastrophizing—expecting the worst and illogically thinking about how awful it would be to miss the putt.

What is a more rational way to approach this situation? The answer is to think realistically about the worst thing that can happen if you miss the putt. When you allow your fears to run wild by catastrophizing, anxiety and tension ensue. When you evaluate the situation rationally, you alleviate your fears. What's the worst thing that can happen if you do miss the putt? You may lose the hole.

You may score one stroke higher for the round. But your friends will still like you, and your family will still love you, and you'll still be alive for tomorrow's activities.

Your worst fears only come true in your mind. The next time you start to pressure yourself, ask yourself realistically what's the worst thing that can happen. Then refocus on making the shot rather than fearing the results.

WHAT DO YOU SAY TO YOURSELF?

Another key to emotional control is what you say to yourself on the golf course. We regularly carry on an inner dialogue or self-talk with ourselves. The content of self-talk varies from person to person. Players who maintain positive self-talk enhance their confidence and feelings of self-worth. Poor self-talk can ruin self-confidence, increase negative thinking, and elevate tension and anxiety.

Most amateur golfers berate themselves when they play poorly. After hitting a ball into the water hazard, they might say to themselves: "You can't hit the fairway if your life depends on it; you're the worst golfer." If a professional hits a ball in the water, he simply sees it as a fluke. Furthermore, one poor shot does not reflect on you as a person. You can be sure Lee Trevino doesn't tell himself what an awful ball striker he is when he hits a poor shot or hits it poorly one day.

Changing negative self-talk to positive self-enhancing statements helps increase confidence and reduce anxiety, but you have to practice it. You begin by identifying your negative self-talk. On a scorecard, monitor your negative thoughts during a round. Write down the negative statement and when it occurs. If you have more negative than neutral or positive thoughts during a round, this indicates that you need to work on changing your self-talk.

TABLE 2
Changing negative self-statements to positive self-statements

Negative Statement	Positive Statement
• I am a lousy putter on bumpy greens.	• Everyone has to putt on the same greens and I'm a good putter.
• Play is so slow, I hate playing in these conditions.	• I'm in no hurry, just relax and enjoy yourself.
• I'm the biggest choker, can't make a putt when it counts.	• I know if I relax and don't get ahead of myself I can make putts when they count.
• This game is so frustrating, I'll never be good enough.	• The challenge of becoming a good player is bouncing back after failure.
• I'm so lazy, why should I even bother to practice.	• I know if I set goals and practice more I can be a better player.

The key is to eliminate negative thoughts and maintain as positive thoughts as you can.
Kelly Gibson, PGA Tour

The next step is to modify your self-talk. Write down the negative self-statements and next to each self-statement, change the negative statement to a positive or at the least a neutral statement (refer to Table 2). For example, change the negative self-statement "you're the worst putter in the world" to "everyone misses a short putt now and then, you have made plenty of putts from that distance."

Change your self-defeating thinking to thoughts that support your self-confidence and feelings of self-worth. The next time you play you'll be more aware of what you say to yourself. By being more aware of what you say to yourself, you can maintain thoughts that help you to play with confidence instead of doubt.

MAKE IT WORK FOR YOU, NOT AGAINST YOU

It was discussed earlier that not all pressure is harmful. The pressure you feel can increase your motivation to practice, help you concentrate better on a difficult shot, and supplies extra energy or adrenaline when you need it. When I give a presentation, the pressure I feel to do a good job for my colleagues can make me prepare better for the presentation. The pressure becomes harmful when I allow myself to worry about the things that may go wrong and begin to get anxious.

How you interpret pressure is a key to dealing with it. You stand over a putt and notice that your heart is pounding and your heart rate has increased. If you think that you are choking or that something is wrong with you, it only further heightens the anxiety. A better way to think is to understand that this is a normal reaction to pressure and that it can help you make the putt. Begin to think of the increase in adrenalin as a positive factor that helps you concentrate better for the putt.

Tour players have learned to interpret pressure as something that is positive or challenging. If they don't get in a pressure situation, they never have a chance to win. It is fun to try to win because you have to win the mental game to win the physical game. Many players like the challenge of dealing with their emotions when they are in contention to win. Depending on how you interpret it, pressure can be perceived as either threatening or challenging, as PGA Tour player Trevor Dodds describes:

> **If you have a chance to win a tournament, that's not pressure. You know your playing well, things are going your way, otherwise you wouldn't be in contention. Pressure is coming down the last hole at Tour School knowing you have to make par to make the cut... I turned it into a challenge and it has made the world of difference because I pulled off a shot that is really, really difficult by turning a threat into a challenge.**

HAVE YOU PREPARED?

Physical and mental preparation is one of the best methods for being ready to handle pressure. Practice and hard work is a valuable source of confidence. Knowing you paid your dues and feeling like you did everything in your power to prepare for competition increases your confidence. The confidence that you gain from preparation and practice is a tremendous way to withstand pressure. Confident players don't fear hitting a bad shot, missing a putt, and don't doubt their ability because they have done everything in their power to prepare for the competition.

> **If you practice enough and get a tremendous amount of confidence—and that's where confidence comes from, it comes from practice—if you practice, you have confidence, then you can withstand pressure.**
> *Lee Trevino (1992)*

If you are confident that you can hit a difficult shot, it is less likely that you get anxious about hitting a bad shot. You have practiced the shot hundreds of times and that feeling helps you to hit the same shot in any situation. A feeling of not being fully prepared to play brings doubt into your game. Doubting your ability to hit a shot breeds anxiety and tension.

REDUCING PHYSICAL TENSION

The best way to maintain an optimal emotional state is to be confident and positive, and not allow your mind to be filled with fear and anxiety. Your thoughts effect your feelings and emotions, and your emotions influence your behavior. When you feel "pressure" that is beyond your ability to cope, you are inviting apprehension and fear into your game. You must approach a pressure situation with determination and confidence that you will prevail. Look at pressure as a challenge to play well rather than an opportunity for failure.

At times, it's hard to realize that your negative thoughts produce anxiety. Sooner or later, anxiety manifests itself as butterflies or sweaty palms, which are easy to identify. Faster identification of the signs of anxiety leads to a faster coping response. The following techniques will help you to reduce unwanted tension and find your optimal zone.

BREATHE THE TENSION AWAY

Controlled breathing is a very simple, effective, and practical method for curtailing worry and reducing physical tension. Mentally, breathing helps focus your attention away from anxiety-producing thoughts by occupying your mind with a simple task. Breathing also triggers a physical relaxation response. When done properly, abdominal breathing increases the amount of oxygen to the blood and carries more energy to the working muscles.

Many athletes breathe improperly when anxious. Breathing is an autonomic function. Under pressure you take shallow breaths. Under extreme pressure, players may hold their breath. Erratic breathing then creates more tension, which leads to poor performance. You must learn to control your breathing when nervous.

You must practice your breathing for it to be effective. Soon, you will be able to integrate breathing into your game during shot preparation. When you practice, you should include three important elements: (1) Take deep breaths through the abdominal cavity (lower stomach); (2) Inhale and exhale slowly and smoothly; and (3) focus your attention on releasing the tension during exhalation. Start by

91

practicing in a relaxed atmosphere and progress up to breathing when anxious (refer to Exercises 1 and 2).

Exercise 1: Rhythmic Abdominal Breathing. Sit or lie down in an area where you won't be distracted. Take a slow, complete breath filling up the lower section of your lungs and then the upper section. Inhale for five seconds, pause, and exhale for five seconds. Concentrate on the rhythm of your breathing and the air filling the lungs. Place one hand on your abdominal region while breathing. If you are breathing correctly, you should feel your hand rise and lower as you inhale and exhale. Slowly and smoothly empty the air completely out of your lungs when exhaling. Focus your attention on reducing muscular tension during the exhalation. Feel the tension drain from your body as you exhale. Practice this breathing exercise for 10 minutes a day for three weeks. When you are comfortable practicing this exercise in a quiet environment, you can do it during your free time in the day, when watching television, riding in a car, waiting in a line, and so on. Then begin to use your breathing when you start to feel anxious or to help you fall asleep.

Exercise 2: Rhythmic Breathing With Cues Words. This exercise is the same as Exercise 1 except you use a cue word during exhalation to help you relax further. Use the same pattern of rhythmic breathing and focus your attention on reducing the tension as you exhale. This is the relaxation phase of the breath. As you exhale repeat a cue word silently to yourself such as "just relax," which helps trigger a relaxation response. You can use any cue word or words that are meaningful to you such as "calm down," "easy," "smooth," or "release." The combination of a cue word and breathing is very effective for reducing tension and focusing your mind away from anxiety producing thoughts.

Once you become proficient at breathing properly, you can begin to use it on the course. Soon, you'll learn to reduce excess tension by taking two or three deep breaths. The best time to use breathing is during your shot preparation (refer to Chapter 7 on applying your psychological skills).

CONSCIOUSLY REDUCE THE TENSION

Most people are not aware of muscular tension that accumulates during the day. Have you ever noticed that at the end of a day your shoulders, back, or neck are sore? Muscular soreness can result from excessive worry that increases muscular tension. First, you must learn to recognize tension before you can begin to consciously release the tension.

One exercise that develops your awareness of muscular tension and helps release tension is progressive relaxation. Progressive relaxation is the process of contracting all the major muscle groups, holding the contraction, and then relaxing the muscles. This process is continued until you have contracted all the major muscle groups in the body (refer to Exercise 3).

Exercise 3: Progressive Relaxation. The purpose of this exercise is to train yourself to recognize when your muscles are tight and when they are relaxed. Find a quiet room and lie down in the corpse position. Take a deep breath and relax. Starting with your right leg, tighten the muscles in that leg by contracting your thigh. Hold the contraction for about eight seconds and release the tension all at once. Notice the difference between a tight muscle and a relaxed muscle. Repeat the process with the same leg. Do the same with the other leg. Move up your body contracting each major muscle group: buttocks, chest, back, shoulders, arms, neck, and facial region.

ON-COURSE TIPS FOR COPING WITH ANXIETY

Anyone knows it's easy to learn to relax in a comfortable environment without distractions or pressure. A true test of a player's ability to control emotions is when she must make a three-foot putt to win a tournament. You must be able to apply what you learned off the course to competitive play. Controlling your emotions is crucial when the heat is on and you have to make birdie on the last hole to win the match. The following are methods that I have found to be the most useful for helping players reduce anxiety and tension on the course.

Slowing down your actions and using positive self-talk helps to counter anxiety.

SLOW DOWN

Anxiety usually causes players to speed up their behaviors on the course. A player walks faster between shots, rushes his shots, and swings faster. Playing under pressure often causes you to speed up your preshot routine to "get a shot over with." Players think that the best way to alleviate the uncomfortable feeling of anxiety is to hurry and get the shot over with as fast as possible. The faster you go, the more anxious you become. This is when you have to consciously slow down everything you do. Don't get caught in a situation where you have to hurry your warm-up. Pace yourself when warming-up. Walk to the first tee more slowly. Take your time walking between each shot. Slow down your preshot routine and be more deliberate without overanalyzing the situation.

> **Whenever I felt the pressure or faced a tough shot [at the 1992 U.S. Open], I said to myself: "Slow down, Tom. Take your time."**
> *Tom Kite (1993), PGA Tour*

BREATH DEEPLY

The nice thing about using breathing to control anxiety is that you can do it at anytime. Breathing is an excellent way to reduce muscular tension and focus your mind on something that doesn't increase your anxiety. If you spend time off the course practicing your breathing exercises, you should learn to relax with just a few deep breaths. You can breath when you're walking to the next shot. Use breathing during your preshot routine to gain the right level of tension for the shot.

STRETCH AWAY THE TENSION

Stretching is another excellent on-course method for reducing tension. For many players, it is hard to notice when they start to become anxious and physically tense. Stretching is not only a good way to check for physical tension, it also has a relaxing effect on the muscles. Stretching brings needed oxygen to tight muscles.

TIGHTEN AND RELEASE THE TENSION

Contracting a tense muscle and releasing the contraction has the same effect as stretching. It is often easier to relax a tight muscle when you fully contract it and then release the tension. You should tighten and release muscle groups that tighten up when you are anxious. If you get tense in the shoulder and neck region, shrug your shoulders to your ears and then release the tension. If it is your arms and hands that tighten up, grip the club tightly and release the tension.

TALK TO YOURSELF

Anxiety increases when a player's self-talk is negative and self-defeating. A player with negative self-talk says: "I'm a choker, there is no way I can make this putt," which increases anxiety and decreases self-confidence. Players have to learn to notice when their self-talk becomes counterproductive and learn to maintain positive self-affirmations. "You're a good putter, you've made this putt thousands of times before" is an example of an affirmation statement that calms you in a pressure situation. Create affirmation statements off the course so you will be prepared the next time you need to give yourself a pep-talk. When you're feeling tense, use your internal coach and give yourself some words of encouragement.

CHANGE YOUR FOCUS

Pressure causes anxiety, and anxiety increase muscular tension. Anxiety and physical tension make you focus internally on the anxiety-producing thought or on changes in your physical state. You then focus internally on your pounding heart, rapid breathing, sweaty palms, and upset stomach, and this further increases anxiety. It puts you on the defensive. Now you know you are anxious and must do something or you'll miss the putt. Not only are you anxious about missing the putt, but you become more anxious about being anxious. Maintaining an internal focus is not a good type of focus for making the putt. At some point you must shift your attention externally to the target. Focus on the line of your putt or the cup, or visualize the ball rolling into the hole.

TAKE YOUR MIND AWAY

Sometimes it helps to escape from a tense situation. You don't have to leave the course, but you can take a trip with your mind. You can visualize a tranquil scene like a beach or a forest. You can imagine yourself in a familiar setting that is relaxing to you. It is similar to daydreaming, but you have a purpose in mind, which is to take a time out from a stressful situation.

LEARN TO ACCEPT IT

The increase in excitement or arousal you experience when under pressure can help in certain ways if you don't let it get out of control. The increase in adrenalin can give you extra energy to hit a bigger drive and concentrate better for your shot. Focusing on how uncomfortable you feel only accelerates your anxiety. Learn to accept it as excitement and use it to your advantage to help you concentrate better or hit a bigger drive. Psych yourself up, not out.

HAVE MORE FUN

Do you get too serious on the golf course so that every shot is a life or death contest? The attitude some players have about their game can cause a great deal of stress. If you place high importance on your game, are more serious, and hate to lose, your game is prone to high anxiety. Shifting your priority to enjoying yourself on the course is a big step but well worth the effort. If your goal is to have fun, there is less pressure to "produce." It's easy to be focused on results when your goal is to win. Focus on the process rather than results. Stressing fun over winning will help to take the monkey off your back.

DEALING WITH FRUSTRATION AND ANGER

The nature of the game of golf causes high frustration for many players. When you ask ex-golfers why they quit playing, they usually reply, "It's too frustrating." It is hard to not be frustrated when you lip out three putts in a row or make a stupid mental error like selecting the wrong club. Hitting one bad shot that spoils a great round can also be devastating.

> **A little bit of anger means you care and are going to play harder, to pay more attention. Uncontrolled anger means you're going to ruin your round.**
> *Tom Kite (1990), PGA Tour*

A controlled anger sometimes is beneficial because it makes you play harder, concentrate more, and gives you a boost of energy. If uncontrolled, frustration or anger leads to overarousal and anxiety. It also causes you to become pessimistic and cynical. If not dealt with, frustration and anger can ruin both your round and your state of mind. Here are some tips for dealing with frustration.

FIND A RELEASE

Sometimes it's hard not to get upset. The key is to gain control before you hit your next shot. The question is, do you try to repress your anger and hold it back or do you vent the anger? Repressing your anger can lead to a big blow-up if you encounter other frustrating situations later. One lip-out is OK, the next one is trying, but a third can lead to a total blowout! It's sometimes more effective to deal with frustration as it occurs. One way is to find a release for your anger, both physically and symbolically. Punish your putter by choking it. Slam the club in the bag and put the shot behind you, or throw your ball in the woods and throw your frustration away. The idea is to release the tension not increase your anger.

PUT IT BEHIND YOU

Frustration is most destructive when you carry it with you to the next shot and it causes you to make poor decisions. It's OK to get mad as long as you don't carry your anger to the next shot. If you're preparing to hit a shot on the 10th tee thinking about how mad you are about the three-putt you hit on nine green, you haven't put it behind you. Sometimes getting mad helps you crush your next tee shot, but it's usually not intentional. Your mind isn't focused in the present. You have to find a way to put the shot behind you. Start thinking about your next shot or call a time out and take your mind off golf for a minute.

ZONE IN, NOT OUT

Frustration usually leads to an increase in anxiety, which takes you out of your optimal zone. If not dealt with, overarousal can hurt you on the shots that follow. You have to use your relaxation skills and get back into your zone. This is when breathing and tensing and releasing your muscles are effective for reducing physical tension. Focusing on your breathing also helps to take your mind away from the anger for a split second, hopefully breaking the frustration chain.

CHAPTER SUMMARY

• Pressure is not always harmful to your play. It can help motivate you to practice, give you extra energy and help you concentrate better for a shot.

• Pressure comes from external sources, but it is how you internalize the pressure that determines if you respond negatively with anxiety or positively with excitement.

• Learning to control your emotions involves understanding what situations pressure you, knowing what happens to you when you become anxious, and learning coping responses.

• Anxiety is often fear about what may or may not happen in the future. Thus, we often become stressed when our minds wander to the future and think about negative consequences. Staying focused in the present and not thinking ahead helps circumvent anxiety.

• Players who are over serious about their game and winning are susceptible to negative emotions. Rearranging your priorities and putting golf in proper perspective can help to alleviate the pressure you put on yourself.

• Practice and preparation are the best way to buffer yourself against anxiety. Confident athletes don't get scared: because they know they can succeed.

• Practice your physical relaxation methods to help your on-course coping when things heat up. Practice abdominal breathing and progressive relaxation to help eliminate physical tension.

• Eventually you must learn to relax in competition. This requires that you have prepared coping strategies for use in the heat of the battle. Some coping responses include slowing down your behavior, breathing, tightening and releasing, stretching, giving yourself a pep talk, and changing your focus.

• All golfers must learn to cope with frustration. Sometimes it is better to deal with it as it surfaces and release the anger before it gets out of control. Learn to put frustration behind and get back into your zone of optimal functioning before you play your next shot.

7

APPLYING YOUR PSYCHOLOGICAL SKILLS: THE PRESHOT ROUTINE

If a routine is in my mind, then it occupies my mind to set-up and to hit the shot. It's kind of like a switch, a mechanism, to get me to concentrate on that specific shot. If I don't have a routine to focus on, then half way through getting ready to hit the shot something may come to mind, and it occasionally does, and I have to back off and force myself back into that routine.

David Edwards, PGA Tour

A player spends as much as four to five hours playing a round of golf, using only a small fraction of that time to mentally prepare for shots and even less time actually hitting shots. In golf, unlike other sports, you have the luxury of playing each shot at your own pace and not playing until you are ready. In reactive sports such as baseball, the batter is forced to play at the pitcher's pace and has to react to the ball whether he is ready or not.

My research and work with pros has taught me that the way you mentally prepare for each shot is critical to achieving optimal performance. During those few seconds before starting your swing, you make crucial decisions, plan and visualize how you will play a shot, program yourself with instructions, and physically prepare your body to execute. Jack Nicklaus believes that 90 percent of good shot making includes two critical factors: how you prepare your mind and the consistency of how you set-up to the target. A shot begins when you start to analyze the requirements of the shot, not when you start your forward press. To achieve optimal performance, you must devise a game plan and use your mind to the best of your ability to prepare for and execute each shot.

This chapter details how to use your mind effectively and prepare positively for each shot. It builds on the last five chapters to show how to integrate your psychological skills into your preshot routine, that is, how to plan, prepare, and program yourself for success during your preshot routine.

LEARN FROM THE PROS

The function of a preshot routine is to integrate your mind and body to create the best shot possible. A preshot routine has three main purposes. First, it helps you process information and make decisions to select a club for the shot. Second, it helps you program yourself to make a good swing. Third, it aids in preparing your mind and body to execute a good swing. If you neglect one of these areas, you fail to fully prepare yourself. Your goal is to train yourself to approach each shot and putt with conviction, confidence, and trust in your ability.

Tour professionals have specific preshot routines they follow that help them prepare for a shot or putt. Tour pros are very systematic and precise in the way they plan and prepare for each shot. Every player prepares differently, but they all try to achieve the same goal—to swing with confidence and trust. Most tour pros have very well-defined, consistent and specific preshot routines that they have developed over years of practice and play.

A preshot routine varies depending on the personality and other preferences of the golfer. Greg Norman, like Jack Nicklaus, prefers a very deliberate preshot routine. Norman selects the shot he wants to play and visualizes that shot by focusing on the apex of the ball in flight. He walks to the ball, aims his clubhead to the target, aligns his body, and sets his grip. He sets his stance, waggles the clubhead back and forth to loosen up, and gets ready for the shot. To trigger his swing, he slides his clubhead away from his body to align the face with the ball.

Chip Beck also uses a very deliberate, mechanical looking

preshot routine. He steps into the ball the same way and looks at the target the same number of times on every shot. A player like Lanny Wadkins takes much less time to prepare for a shot. He pulls the club from the bag, sets-up to the ball, looks at the target, and goes. He feels more comfortable taking less time. John Daly is also a player who prefers to take less time over the ball. If you have ever watched Daly putt, it looks like he is in a hurry to get to his next shot. He simply selects the putt he wants to hit, sets up next to the ball, takes one quick practice swing, sets up over the ball, looks at the hole once and goes.

---

*All tour pros have a personal
style of preparing for a shot,
but each player is consistent with
how they approach a shot.*

Each player has a unique style of preparation. The common denominator is that each player has a routine he or she believes in and they follow that routine whether they are leading a tournament or in last place. The pace, deliberateness, and specific behaviors in your preshot routine depend on your personality and what feels comfortable to you. For example, a very aggressive player like Lanny Wadkins has a very short, quick preshot routine. A conservative, calculated player like Jack Nicklaus uses a slower, deliberate routine.

PROCESSING INFORMATION AND PLANNING THE SHOT
CHECKING YOUR STATUS

If a friend blindfolded you, walked you on to a green, set you up over a ball, and asked you to make the putt, how confident would you feel about making a putt? Probably not very confident. The first step in preparing for any shot begins by evaluating the information in the environment so that you can decide how to proceed. A tee shot, for example, requires you to process several pieces of information including the layout of the hole, the direction of the wind, the distance you want to hit the ball, and where you want to be to approach the green. This information is critical for making a decision about the right club to hit and the direction you want to start the ball.

With an approach shot, before you even begin to select a club you must check the lie of the ball, compute the distance to the target, check the wind speed and direction, estimate how far the ball will fly and roll given the conditions, and decide where to aim your shot. Putting is no different. There is an art to reading greens that requires you to gather several pieces of information, fit them into the puzzle, and select a course of action. You must check the slope speed, firmness of the green, judge the distance to the hole, factor in the effects of the wind, moisture, and grain on the green, and then select a line and speed in which to hit the ball.

Good players instinctively analyze the situation. Professionals know what to look for, make the best decision given the available information, and rely on their instincts and experience.

BE SURE ABOUT YOUR DECISIONS

After you have assessed the requirements of a shot, the next step is to plan the shot. If you neglect this step, you won't be able to make a positive, determined swing. To plan a shot, you must select a club, a target, and the type of shot you want to hit. The type of shot you hit and club you use for the shot depend upon each other. The type of shot (low, high, fade, draw, etc.) dictates which club you select, given the distance to the target (i.e. a high fade won't travel as far as a low draw given the same club and conditions).

The most critical factor is being positive about the club you have selected. You must be convinced that you have the right club to get the job done, otherwise you won't allow yourself to swing aggressively or decisively at the ball. You can't make a smooth and determined swing if you're thinking that you have too much or not enough club. What happened the last time you were unsure about what club to hit? You switched back and forth between two clubs searching for the right one, never coming to a real decision. As a result, your swing was choppy and hesitant because you lacked confidence in the club you selected.

Being certain about the club you selected
leads to a confident swing.

Many good players often neglect to pick a target, which is a very important part of the preparation for any shot. When you align yourself for a tee shot, do you set-up on the fairway in general or do you pick a specific tree in the background of the fairway? Give your body precise information to respond to by selecting a specific target in the background. When you don't pick a specific target, you send a message to yourself that you hope to get the ball somewhere on the fairway.

Experienced golfers usually have several shots they can play for any given situation. Typically, the situation dictates the type of shot that a player feels comfortable hitting. If you naturally fade the ball and a shot calls for a fade around the corner of a dogleg, you intuitively will see that as the right type of shot for you to hit. Once you select a fade for the shot, don't second guess yourself or change your mind in favor of another shot. Remember that the purpose of a preshot routine is to help you swing free and decisively, and reduce any doubt about club selection, target, or type of shot to hit (refer to Chapter 5: "Learning to Let it Go").

> **You can go through all the physical preparation you want but if you are undecided when you get up over the ball or undecided on what you want to do or have any doubt, then you are going to hit a bad shot.**
> *NCAA Division I Golfer*

Putting is no different. If you think that your read the putt incorrectly, your stroke will usually be jerky and controlled. The biggest error I see with amateur golfers is a change of mind about what a putt is going to do, sometimes in mid-stroke. But this can happen at any stage. What often happens is that you read a putt to break a certain amount, then when you get over it, you don't think it will break as much, so you decelerate the putter at the last second in an attempt to hit it softer, which results in a tentative, miss-hit putt. Changing your mind creates doubt, and doubt creates indecision about how to stroke the ball. Carry out your first instinct and first read of the putt, and don't change your mind. Eliminate indecision so that you can focus your energy on allowing yourself to make a good swing.

Once you have chosen the line to hit the ball on, go with it. Focus on the line as you approach the ball and don't lose sight of it. The line will visually look different from over the ball, but stay focused on your line and don't overreact and overread the putt.

PROGRAM YOURSELF FOR SUCCESS
LOCK YOUR MIND INTO THE TASK

> **I think a routine helps when things are going bad. It is always something that you can focus all your attention on and not have it hurt and not be focusing on mechanics or focusing on your score.**
> *NCAA Division I Golfer (Cohn, 1991)*

Having a specific routine to follow helps you know what to focus on and when. It is easier to focus in the present and harder for your mind to wander when you know exactly what you're supposed to do and when you should do it. When you have learned to prepare for a shot by visualizing the flight of the ball, taking a practice swing, setting-up to the target, and waggling and glancing twice at the target, you positively lock in your attention. When you have something specific to focus on, it's harder for your attention to be diverted by negative thoughts.

---

*A preshot routine aids concentration by keying you
to what you should focus on for a good shot.*

Indecision at the last moment may cause you to hit a poor putt.

Having a specific routine also helps you know when you are not concentrating. When you deviate from your normal preshot behaviors, it's a sign that you're either distracted by something or just being lazy with your preparation. When Scott Hoch missed a three-foot putt to win the Masters, many people claimed he took too much time to analyze and prepare for the shot, which altered his normal preparation. David Edwards told me that a preshot routine is as much a part of the shot as the swing itself. He uses his routine not only to help him concentrate but also as a way of refocusing his attention when distracted. He said:

> Sometimes I get up over the ball and my mind wanders to something else. I'll say, "What in the world are you thinking about?"... The routine is a way to help me concentrate. I know specifically what I am going to do when I get up over the shot. If I don't have a routine, it's easy for my mind to wander because there's really no direction to what I am going to do, I don't really know what I am going to do, I don't know if I'm going to waggle two or three times... So to me it's a form of concentration to have a set routine and get up and do it, it's all a part of the stroke to me.

You must first develop a specific preshot routine to follow, then become aware when you are not concentrating for the shot. When you learn to recognize that you're not focused on your routine, you can refocus and lock-in your mind on the task.

THE POWER OF IMAGINATION

Many high-handicap golfers doom themselves before they ever swing the club because of the negative images that fill their mind when preparing for a shot. A negative thinker dwells on the problems that the shot presents (water hazards, bunkers, high rough) and how to avoid the trouble. When you think about what not to do, negative images pass through your mind—the ball hooking out-of-bounds or the ball slicing into the water. These images make you defensive from the start. The first reaction is to avoid the water, stay away from the out-of-bounds, evade the bunker. The fear and anxiety then controls your swing.

The mind can be either powerfully pessimistic or powerfully optimistic, depending on how you choose to use it. The more focused you are with your preparation, the more you can make a confident swing. A first step in programming yourself for any shot begins with a clear positive mental picture of what you want to do. Most tour professionals automatically use their imagination to set-up the type of shot they want to hit, or to select a line to hit their putt. Greg Norman (1988) states: "I visualize the precise shot I want to play. I see the ball leaving my clubface, arching into the sky, and coming down next to the target." Imagining or visualizing the type of shot you want to play (or line of a putt) is a powerful tool to help set-up the type of shot you want to hit and to help execute the shot. Visualizing the ball landing in the middle of the fairway is much more comforting than picturing it splashing in the water; it provides your body with a positive image.

Imagination goes beyond just seeing the flight of the ball. Seeing the ball fly to your target is the first step to programming yourself for a particular shot. To go to the next level, you need to translate that positive visual image of the shot into an image with which your body can relate. Imagination includes both visual images and "feeling" images. Your body responds to both visual and kinesthetic (feeling) images. The memory of the feeling of a perfectly struck shot is an example of a feeling or "sensation" image. This type of image is extremely powerful for programming yourself for action.

After seeing a positive visual image of the shot, recall the feeling of a perfectly struck ball from a similar situation in the past. What do you think of when you recall the feeling of a good shot? Do you think about your balance, the tempo of the swing, or the feeling of making solid contact with the ball? Use an image that you can bring to life. Recall the feeling of a well-struck ball and program yourself for success.

PREPARE LIKE THE PROS
START YOUR ENGINE

Golf is different from other sports when you think about how much "down" time there is between shots. The fluctuating amount of time spent between shots makes it especially difficult to get into a good rhythm or flow of play. Many players I work with have a difficult time finding a rhythm when play is slow.

You not only have to prepare your mind, but you also have to "warm-up" your body to prepare for shots. If you're the first to hit off the tee and the last to hit your approach shot, you might wait 10 minutes between shots before you hit your next one. After 10 minutes the body cools down rapidly like the engine of a car and is not ready to run at peak efficiency until it is warmed-up. A good preshot routine helps you to refocus your mind and warm-up your engine for the shot.

> **Controlling the pace and number of my waggles and the number of times I look at the hole promotes a tempo that will help my swing work at its best.**
> *Tom Kite (1990), PGA Tour*

This is why the physical components of a preshot routine are so important. Taking a practice swing, aligning and setting-up to a target, and waggling the club all help to get you into your optimal zone to prepare your body for action. A practice swing has two purposes. It helps to warm-up the body for action by loosening the muscles and priming the sensory pathways that will be used in the actual swing. A practice swing also helps you recall a specific feeling of the shot you want to hit. If the shot calls for a fade, you can use a practice swing to help you recall the feeling of a fade and program yourself for the upcoming shot.

Waggling the club is an excellent way to make a transition from thinking about the shot to executing the shot. Waggling the club has two purposes. First, it is a means of checking for physical tension and keeping the muscles loose for the swing. Second, waggling the club is used for mirroring the tempo of your swing, and thus programming your swing tempo.

Do You Believe?

Seeing and feeling the shot you want to hit is very important to programming yourself for the shot. After selecting a shot you want to play and programming yourself for the shot, do you always believe that you will hit your target? It is easy to "see" a good shot, but seeing a good shot is very different from thinking you will hit a good shot. When working with golfers, I always tell them that they have to take the next step and go beyond picturing the ball fly to the target by knowing that the ball is going to the target.

Go beyond seeing a good shot by truly believing you will hit a good shot.

"I know this shot is going right for the pin."

This requires that you be realistic with your perception of what you believe you can do. You must accurately assess your ability and skill level. Don't expect to hit the ball five feet from the pin on every shot if your skills are not up to the task. If a good shot for you is 30 feet from the pin, then you can realistically expect you will do that.

Your confidence on any given shot is influenced in part by how you are playing that day (refer to Chapter 6 on Confidence). If you miss six putts in a row, you probably talk yourself into thinking that you'll miss the next putt like most amateurs do. That's why when you begin to play poorly, your play gets even worse. When you expect to continue to putt poorly, and unless you make a couple of putts in a row, you fulfill this expectation and keep missing putts.

You must believe you're going to make your next putt regardless of what happened on the last putt. If you miss six putts in a row, you must convince yourself that the chance of making the next putt has increased. You may indeed have a mechanical problem preventing you from making your best stroke, but you don't want to compound the problem by thinking you are going to miss.

> **Just get into the hole and let if flow. There's only two things that can happen—you either make it or miss it.**
> *Tim Simpson, PGA Tour*

ARE YOU FREE?

The major intention of a preshot routine is to help you feel comfortable over the ball when it is time to swing the club. It is easier to be comfortable when you are confident with the club you selected, the shot you want to hit, your set-up and alignment to the target, and when you think positively about the shot. If you have any doubt about one of these areas, you reduce your trust when it's time for you to start the club back. If you're not comfortable when it's time to execute, then your routine was ineffective at some point or you were not focused on the process of preparation.

---

*You will make your best
swing when your mind is free
of doubt and indecision.*

That is why the preliminary steps of a routine are so important to calming your mind and letting yourself hit a good shot. Have you ever noticed just before you started your swing that you suddenly wondered if you had the right club for the shot or thought that you weren't aligned well? At this point you have not only lost your image and feeling of a good shot, but you're not free to make a good swing. Freeing yourself to make a good swing requires that you put all doubt aside and be confident in your decisions. Trust that you can make a good swing.

Freeing your mind also demands that you have faith in your ability to hit your target. When the pressure starts to mount and you feel a loss of control, the tendency is to control your swing mechanically. You block your dominant response (a free unmechanical swing) because you give your body technical instructions. Most golfers use one or two swing cues to initiate the swing. When you get anxious or doubt your ability, you tend to use multiple mechanical swing thoughts to guide your swing through its path.

The final step in freeing your mind is to give up conscious control of your swing and let yourself do what you have practiced (refer to Chapter 4 on "Learning To Let It Flow"). This is not the time to give yourself technical instructions. The more complicated you make it, the harder it is for you to free yourself to swing automatically. You plan, prepare, then involve yourself with the cues in the environment allowing you to react to your target.

Simplify the final thoughts in your routine. Pick one swing cue that does not involve mechanical instructions; think about swing tempo rather than making sure your club is parallel at the top of the swing. Focus on the target rather than on what your body is doing during the swing. D.A. Weibring describes how doing his homework for each shot allows him to "dissolve" into his target and react:

> **You can't be thinking about eight different [mechanical] things. You've just got to pick your shot, make your decision, trust it, and go... All your homework starts at the very beginning and it works itself up to a peak. So it builds all the way and the last couple seconds you're standing back here or wherever you see your shot, as you walk into it, you're ready to go. Everything should dissolve and you just hit the shot... But you have to prepare yourself for what you want to do and then react to it.**

TUNING-UP AND STAYING IN CONTROL

A preshot routine is a good way to deflect pressure and counter anxiety. It is harder to stay focused in the present when the pressure is on. Pressure forces you to think about results. When you think about results (or negative outcomes), your anxiety increases.

This is when having a specific routine to follow helps you deal with the anxiety. When you starting thinking negatively or feel anxious, sticking to a specific routine helps you refocus your mind on the process of hitting a good shot. Usually, anxiety causes you to speed-up your normal actions, including your preparation for a shot and the tempo of your swing. Refocusing your attention on your preshot behaviors reduces anxiety and negative thoughts. David Edwards feels that anxiety forces him out of his normal rhythm. Having a routine to stick to helps him counter the negative effects of anxiety:

> **It's very easy when you get anxious to take more time to do whatever, and those things for the most part are negative. They let bad thoughts in, they get you out of your normal rhythm and routine, they change the way you normally go about something and I think that's generally bad. So I think a routine and forcing yourself to learn to stick to your routine—get up, ready or not, here it comes and hit the shot even though you don't feel like you're ready—is better and in time you will learn. And I feel like I perform better than if I try to wait until I'm ready because you won't ever get ready and you'll get to where you can't ever get ready. It gets worse instead of better. I think a routine is a good way to combat some of the anxiety.**

When you first start to feel tense, this is an excellent time to use the relaxation techniques described in Chapter 6. Two excellent methods of relaxing yourself when preparing for shots is abdominal breathing and tightening and releasing your muscles. If you watch professional basketball players at the free throw line, you see them take a slow, deep breath to settle into the shot before they shift attention to the rim. Breathing can be used to clear your mind at the start of your preshot routine and for eliminating excess muscular tension. Deep breathing is an excellent means of reducing excess tension in the shoulder and neck region, especially for putting.

The start of the preshot routine is an excellent time to use breathing to relax.

Contracting and then relaxing a particular muscle group also is effective for reducing excess muscular tension. You can reduce tension in your arms and hands by fully tightening your hands on the grip and then releasing. This technique can be used for any muscle group that is tense. If you shoulders tighten when putting, shrug your shoulders and fully contract the muscles in that area for about six seconds and then release the tension. Often, you must fully contract a muscle to reduce muscular tension in that area.

114

Besides tensing-up, pressure causes you to change your behaviors on the golf course. Usually, you do everything faster when under pressure including a hurried preshot routine. Too much pressure causes anxiety, which is an unpleasant feeling for most people. This feeling of uneasiness causes a player to think "hurry up and just finish the shot" to restore order. The excess rush of adrenaline you get when your excited has the same effect: you speed up the normal pace of your preshot behaviors.

> **Pressure creates tension, and when you're tense, you want to get the task over and done with as fast as possible. The more you hurry in golf, the worse you probably will play, which leads to even heavier pressure and greater tension.**
> *Jack Nicklaus (Ferguson, 1972), PGA Tour*

Make a conscious effort to slow down your preshot behaviors when you notice that your are anxious. Take enough time to analyze the situation and plan and prepare for the shot. Slow down how fast you walk up to the ball to set-up and between shot. Take your usual amount of time with your alignment and set-up. Consciously relax your arms and hands when you waggle the club. Counter the pressure by maintaining a normal pace with your routine and keeping positive thoughts to insure that you're fully prepared for the shot.

DEVELOPING A PRESHOT ROUTINE

I discussed earlier that how you prepare for a shot is influenced by your personality. Players such as Lanny Wadkins and John Daly choose to play fast because that's what feels most comfortable to them. Other players like Chip Beck and Jack Nicklaus are deliberate because they feel more comfortable making absolutely sure they are ready. The pace of your preshot preparation also depends on how complex or simple you choose to make your routine. The more ingredients in your routine, the more complex it will be, and the longer it will take. The more simple your routine, the faster it is, and also the easier it is for you to follow.

How you approach each shot mentally also will depend upon your personal style. If you primarily learn by pictures and respond better to visual images, you should use those images to

115

your advantage. Your mental rehearsal should comprise visual images of the flight of the ball and pictures of how you will achieve that shot. See yourself swinging with control and good tempo.

If you learn more through physical feelings and respond more to sensations you pick up from your body, use those images to help you prepare for the shot. Your mental rehearsal should include the feeling of what you are trying to accomplish. You should focus more on the feeling of good tempo or the feeling of a well-struck ball, such as the feeling of a solid hit at impact. The last option is to use both visual and feeling images if you relate to both styles of information processing.

KEEP A GOOD RHYTHM

A preshot routine should feel comfortable to you. You shouldn't have to struggle with making yourself do it. When you first change the way you prepare for and approach a shot, it's harder to get into a rhythm and feel comfortable with the "new" routine. The same thing happens when you make a mechanical swing change. At first the new change doesn't feel right, but with practice you begin to feel comfortable with the change.

If you play you best when focused on a target, focusing harder on your routine may hinder your performance because you lose sight of the target or your goal. For some players, focusing more on their routine than the goal has a positive effect. If you have difficult time eliminating negative thoughts, focusing intensely on your routine helps to take your mind off the negative thought.

A routine should ultimately be automatic, like a well-grooved swing; something that you do without awareness. At first, when doing your routine you must consciously think about completing the new routine. It takes time for a new routine to become ingrained in your memory to the point where you don't consciously think about it. This requires that you spend time practicing your new routine until it becomes automatic.

> **The more we ingrain a routine and rhythm of setting-up by repeatedly rehearsing our procedures on the driving range and in our casual play, the less we'll be likely to step out of line when it really matters.**
> *Seve Ballesteros (1988), PGA Tour*

A routine should have a good pace and rhythm from start to finish. Once you pull the club out of the bag and begin to plan the shot, your routine should flow into the swing without interruption. You interrupt the flow and rhythm of the routine when you become distracted, lose your focus, or stop in the middle. Inactivity itself breaks the pace of the routine. One big fault of amateur golfers is "freezing" over the ball before they pull the club back. The frozen golfer is waiting for someone to start his backswing for him. This is called paralysis by overanalysis. The golfer is (1) trying to remember all the mechanical instructions from his or her teacher; (2) paralyzed by the fear of hitting a bad shot; or (3) has not developed a trigger that automatically initiates the swing. The inactivity in the routine breads further indecisiveness and doubt.

> **A brisk pace helps breed confidence. One fault many players get into is the incessant fiddling and fidgeting during the address. It seems to me that they're second-guessing themselves at a time when they should be absolutely confident and ready to swing.**
> *Greg Norman (1988), PGA Tour*

Whenever you break the flow of your routine, stop yourself, refocus your mind, and start over from the beginning. David Edwards learned to be aware when he deviates from his routine. He catches himself and starts his preparation over form the beginning. David said: "If I'm lost in the middle [of the routine] or I realized I haven't gone through my routine, I step back and go through the entire routine because that's as much a part of the stroke."

BE CONSISTENT BUT NOT COMPULSIVE

> **If you watch a guy that is playing good, in what I call the zone, he is doing everything the same, the amount of time he takes [to prepare] is the same, the swing looks the same because he feels comfortable and confident.**
> *Bob Tway, PGA Tour*

A preshot routine allows you to prepare for each shot or putt

117

consistently. Erratic preparation leads to inconsistent performance. Your thoughts and images, how you align to the target, and your practice swings should be identical from shot to shot and putt to putt. Consistency in the physical part of your preparation (using practice swings, aligning to the target, waggling the club, etc.) helps you to keep your thoughts and images consistent.

If the physical part of your routine is set and you do the same thing repeatedly, it doesn't allow room for changing your thoughts when you are over the ball. The physical helps to maintain the mental part. Deviating from the physical routine alters your mental routine and invites more doubt. It is easier to change your decisions when you alter the physical part of the routine by taking more time, more practice swings.

You should strive to prepare consistently for each shot and putt, yet not be compulsive about doing your routine perfectly. Golfers who think too much about doing a perfect routine lose their focus on hitting a good shot. It is the same as focusing so hard on the line of your putt that you lose the feel for the distance and leave the putt three-feet short. Your goal is not to be perfect in how you approach each shot, rather, your goal is to prepare your mind and body for making a good swing.

Don't become so dependent on your routine that you think you will hit a bad shot without it.

What happens when you find yourself in a situation where you can't do your normal routine—when it's raining hard or very windy? It becomes a problem when you think you'll hit a bad shot when you don't do your routine. If you become too dependent on your routine and find yourself in a situation where you can't or didn't do it, this can only create doubt and take your focus away from the shot. Develop a preshot routine and strive to do your routine consistently, but don't be alarmed when you cannot or haven't done your routine.

EXAMPLES OF PRESHOT ROUTINES

The following are examples of specific preshot routines for full shots, putting, and chipping. They're intended to be a guide for you to develop you own style of preparing for each type of shot. The thoughts and images you use will depend on your personal preference of processing information. How many practice swings you use, the number of times you waggle the club and look at the target will vary depending on what feels right for you.

PRESHOT ROUTINE FOR FULL SHOTS

Stage of Preshot Routine	Psychological Skill
1. Select a club and type of shot based on specifics of the shot.	1. Take time to make sure of your decisions and don't second-guess yourself.
2. Step behind the ball and select a specific target.	2. Take a deep breath to adjust arousal level.
3. Align the ball with the target from behind ball and/or take a practice swing.	3. Imagine the ball flying to the target and identify with the feeling of a perfect shot from the past.
4. Approach the ball to set-up and align.	4. Reassure yourself that you will hit a good shot, say, "you've hit this shot a thousand times before."
5. Set-up and align club and body to the target.	5. Focus on the target and/or focus on a swing key such as "smooth tempo."
6. Make final adjustments, waggle the club, and glance at target.	6. Relax and feel the tempo of the swing. Trust you will make a good swing.

PRESHOT ROUTINE FOR PUTTING

Stage of Preshot Routine	Psychological Skill
1. Step behind the ball and assess the slope of green, distance from target, etc.	1. Take a deep breath to adjust arousal level and clear mind.
2. Align the ball with the target from behind ball.	2. Imagine the ball rolling on your intended line with the correct speed.
3. Approach the ball to set-up.	3. Believe that you will make the putt and tell self "you made this putt many times." Keep a positive image in mind.
4. Take a practice swing(s) next to the ball.	4. Feel the tempo of the swing that matches the speed or pace of the actual putt.
5. Set-up and align putter face and body to the target.	5. Focus on the line of the putt.
6. Make final adjustments and glance at the target.	6. Loosen grip pressure and feel the tempo of swing. Trust yourself to make a good stroke.

PRESHOT ROUTINE FOR FULL SHOTS

Stage of Preshot Routine	Psychological Skill
1. Assess the lie of the ball, the slope of green, distance from target, etc.	1. Take a deep breath to adjust arousal level and clear the mind.
2. Align the ball with the target from behind ball.	2. Pick a spot to land the ball, see the ball landing on that spot and breaking towards the hole.
3. Approach the ball to set-up.	3. Believe that you will make a good shot and say "you can make this shot." Keep a positive image in mind.
4. Take practice swings next to the ball.	4. Decide on the tempo of swing that will achieve the shot.
5. Set-up and align clubface and body to the target.	5. Focus on the trajectory and line of the chip.
6. Make final adjustments and glance at target.	6. Loosen grip pressure and feel the tempo of swing. Trust yourself to make a good swing.

Chapter Summary

• The ultimate purpose of a preshot routine is to help you be confident, focused, and free on all shots and putts.

• Be sure to use all information available to you to help you plan your shot. When you decide how to play the shot, don't second-guess yourself and change your mind at the last second. Stick with what your instincts tell you.

• Use your preshot routine to help you focus on what it takes for you to make a good swing. If you notice that you are not focusing on your preparation for the shot, refocus on your routine.

• Imagine what you want to do with the shot to program yourself. See the shot you want to hit in vivid detail and translate that image into a feeling to which your body can relate.

• The most critical part of preparing for a shot is to allow yourself to swing freely without reservation or controlling the path of the club. Instead of thinking mechanics, feel how you want to hit the ball using your practice swing. Then focus on a general swing thought that will allow your body to take over.

• When you feel pressure, that is the time to focus intensely on the process and ingredients of your routine to squeeze out negative thoughts and eliminate anxiety. Slow down your pace to what seems slower than your normal pace.

• Each player will have a different method of preparing for a shot, depending on their personality and personal characteristics. Develop a routine that is suited best to your style of play and your mannerisms.

• Your routine should have a good pace overall. If you are distracted, lose focus, or entertain a negative thought, stop and refocus. When you are sidetracked, start your routine over from the beginning.

• Be consistent with your preshot thoughts and behaviors from shot to shot and putt to putt. Consistent preparation leads to consistent performance. Don't be so dependent on your routine that if you are unable to do your normal routine, you assume you'll hit a bad shot.

8

PRACTICE LIKE THE PROS: IMPROVING THE QUALITY OF PRACTICE

BY DR. PATRICK J. COHN & DR. PEGGY RICHARDSON

> All my life I've tried to hit practice shots with great care. I try to have a clear-cut purpose in mind on every swing. I always practice as I intend to play. And I learned long ago that there is a limit to the number of shots you can hit effectively before losing your concentration on your basic objectives.
> *Jack Nicklaus (1974), PGA Tour*

The time you spend on the practice tee and green is proportional to the improvements you make in your game, but only if it is quality practice. Improving the quality of practice is an important area that has been neglected by instructors and golf psychologists. Many amateur golfers think that mindlessly hitting 50 drives as far as they can is good practice. Good exercise, yes, effective practice, no. Getting the most out of your practice means giving complete attention to each shot. As Jack Nicklaus said, you should practice with the intention of improving an area of your game and maximizing transfer to the course, rather that just smashing balls as far as possible.

Improving the quality of your practice means practicing in a way that best transfers what you learn to on-course situations. This includes hitting shots in a variety of conditions similar to those you encounter on the golf course. Healthy practice also involves varying your practice by switching clubs often and practicing different types of shots in a variety of situations. The best practice is practice that quickens learning and directly relates to your play on the golf course.

In line with the theme of this book, it is also important to combine your mental-skills training with your physical practice so you can readily use your mental skills to achieve optimal performance on the golf course.

Unlike the pros, most amateur players don't have a lot of time to practice and improve their game. Other commitments at home, work, or school make it impossible for the occasional golfer to spend two or more hours per day practicing. This makes quality practice even more important for the player with limited practice time. Thus, whether your play golf for a hobby or play for a living, learning how to use your practice time effectively should be a priority, especially if you have trouble finding enough time to practice.

QUALITY PRACTICE MAKES PERFECT PRACTICE

The saying "practice makes perfect" is not entirely true unless you're totally focused during practice and achieve quality practice. Most high-handicap golfers think that just going to the practice tee and hitting golf balls one after another on the range is good practice. This may be effective for loosening-up prior to a round but it does little to enhance learning or future performance.

Each time you hit a ball, you should focus on accomplishing something specific, and be totally immersed in that purpose. Your goal can be as simple as checking your ball position on each shot or as complicated as working on making a major mechanical change. The skills you work on during practice vary depending upon (1) your skill level and the amount of time you devote to practice; (2) whether you are making a mechanical change or grooving the fundamentals of your swing; or (3) whether it's preround practice for competition, or practice to improve your game.

Tour pros have already mastered the fundamentals of the swing. When pros practice, they work on fine tuning the swing and making minor adjustments. Casual golfers usually practice the fundamentals of the swing (stance, posture, grip, backswing, downswing, and so on). Thus, the level of skill and the amount of time you have to practice dictates the purpose of your practice.

It doesn't matter whether you are a low or high handicap player, when you practice, you should have a specific idea of what you are trying to improve. You should know what the correct move feels like and how it looks, and what the wrong move feels like and how it looks. You can use a video camera, step in front of a mirror, or ask an instructor to give you some feedback.

One step at a time. Whether you are grooving your swing or working on technique, your mind can only hold one thought at a time. It's impossible to think about your grip pressure, posture, and plane of your swing at the same time. Thus, it's important to develop good practice habits and limit your work to making one specific change in your swing at a time. After you have mastered a particular change (posture during the swing), move to the next area you want to improve. Later you can put the pieces together into a complete whole, which is vital for transferring what you have learned to the golf course.

Work on one area at a time because the mind can only process one thought at a time.

Many teachers break down the swing into manageable parts (i.e., the take away, body turn, position at the top, etc.) to change part of a player's swing that needs improvement. Then those parts must be put together to form a complete swing. If improving a part of your swing (take away) doesn't transfer to the improving your entire swing, then you're not practicing efficiently. Each part in the golf swing influences another part: the swing is a chain reaction. Eventually the parts of the swing must be integrated into a complete swing.

How you practice changes depending on the purpose of your practice. A player who wants to groove an already solid swing should practice with the goal of focusing more on tempo and repeating the swing. A player who wants to improve the mechanics of her swing, should focus on changing one part at a time and how each part relates to the entire swing.

Practice or preround preparation? How you practice and

what you work on depends on whether you are preparing to play a round of golf or if you are practicing to improve your game. Practice prior to a round should be just a warm-up rather than a "practice session." The major goal of preround practice is to loosen and warm-up your muscles. It is also a time to find your rhythm and develop a good tempo for play that day.

Another goal of preround practice is to find a shot pattern that you can trust for the day. A shot pattern is the consistency of ball flight from shot to shot. For example, if you normally fade the ball from left to right, can you be confident that flight pattern will happen on the course from what you experience in warm-up?

For preround practice, it's too late at this point to make a mechanical change in your swing. Changing or fixing your swing before a round can actually hurt your game. You won't correct the problem in the limited time you have, and you certainly won't be able to ingrain the change in your memory. The best you can do at that point is to find a swing key that helps you produce a consistent pattern with your shots for that day. If you have a good idea of the pattern of your shots, you can play that shot for the day and later work on making a swing change.

Thus, quality practice is giving your complete attention to what you are doing and having a specific purpose in mind for each shot you hit. This means taking the time to think before you rake another ball over to hit. You should have specific goals each time you go out to practice, and tailor that practice to what you are trying to accomplish. The amount of time spent or number of shots hit are never as important as specific quality practice.

WHAT ARE YOU WORKING ON?

Having specific goals for practice helps direct your attention to what you need to improve. Goals also help peak your interest, maintain your persistence, and give you a sense of accomplishment when you have achieved a goal. There are two different types of practice goals. The first is physical performance goals. These are goals you set for improving the quality of your putting stroke and swing technique. Making a mechanical swing change, working on your swing tempo, or generally focusing on the movement pattern of your swing

125

are examples of areas that can be used to formulate physical performance goals.

The second type is outcome goals, which relate to the quality of the results of your performance. Examples of outcome goals include how many putts in a row you can make from three feet, hitting seven of 10 nine-irons to within 30 feet of the target, or hitting four of five drivers into a specified target area. It is easier to evaluate whether you have achieved an outcome goal than a performance goal.

Performance and outcome goals. The type of goals you set, physical performance goals or outcome goals, depends on your level of skill. Physical performance goals deal with the mechanics of your swing or how the swing feels or looks to you. A problem with physical performance goals is that it's hard to evaluate your progress because you don't receive clear-cut feedback about how well you are doing unless you have an instructor continuously watching you. Achieving your goal depends on the changes you feel in your swing, feedback your teacher gives you, or changes you see in your actual play. Thus, when you set goals to improve your swing technique, I recommend that you set your goals based on the amount of time you want to devote to working on each one.

Let's say you're working on keeping your wrists firm in your putting stroke. Ultimately your objective is to have firm wrists when putting. You then devise a goal that helps you to achieve your objective. Your goal might be to spend 10 minutes a day at home putting on the carpet (or at the course) keeping your wrist firm. The goal is not to make the putt, it is to focus on keeping your wrist fixed when you stroke the ball. If you spend 10 minutes a day working on your stroke, you have achieved your goal. When you can consistently keep your wrists firm without thinking about it, the change is ingrained in your memory and you have achieved your objective.

Outcome goals are easier to evaluate than goals used for changing technique.

126

Outcome goals are much easier to evaluate than performance goals because you have a specific, measurable goal and you get clear feedback about how you are doing. It's also easier to set specific outcome goals. Let's use the example of putting again. Say your putting mechanics are sound and you want to groove your putting stroke. Instead of working on the mechanics of the stroke, your goal is to make five out of 10 putts from 10 feet away. In this case, you know exactly what the task is and you get instant and clear feedback about how well you are doing. Using outcome goals help to keep you involved in practice drills because they maintain your persistence until you attain your goal. Outcome goals can be set for any area of your game that you want to improve.

Guidelines for setting goals. The following are general guidelines for setting your practice goals:

1. Set goals that you can realistically reach based on your present skill level. You don't want to get discouraged with goals that are too difficult to attain. If you can't reach a practice goal you set for that day, it is too difficult.

2. Goals should not be too easy either. Set challenging mini-goals in practice that will motivate you to do your best. Goals that are too easy won't maintain your interest, nor help your progress.

3. Use specific or measurable goals so you can easily see how you are progressing. Instead of saying, "My goal is to make as many putts as I can today," say, "My goal is to make 25 three-foot putts in a row before I leave today."

4. Focus on daily mini-goals but also have an idea of your long-term objectives. One goal for the day might be to make three putts (out of 10 attempts) from 10 feet, but your long term objective may be to be able to sink five putts (out of 10 attempts) from 10 feet by the end of the month.

5. Give yourself a certain time to attain your goal. For chipping, a goal you could set is to chip-in a ball from 20 feet from the pin in 10 minutes. If it only takes eight minutes, the next time try to do it in fewer that eight minutes.

6. Focus on the positive instead of the negative. Instead of saying, "My goal is not to shank any balls today," say, "My goal is to hit these practice balls on the center of the clubface."

7. Provide a way to get clear feedback about goal attainment. If it's difficult to tell how you are progressing, ask for assistance or use another form of feedback available to you. Many tour professionals travel with a video camera, which gives them better feedback about how they are progressing. Use some type of feedback that allows you to see how your are progressing.

8. Revise and reset your goals often. Once you attain a practice goal, make the goal more difficult the next time. If you reached a goal of making 10 out of 20 sand saves, the next time make your goal more difficult.

9. Maintain your commitment to your goals by rewarding yourself for achieving a goal.

10. Set both physical performance goals and outcome goals.

Practice Like You Play

Many golfers fail to practice in a way that transfers what they learn to actual on-course play. I often hear players, both amateur and professional, say that they can hit the ball great on the range but can't take their practice game to the golf course. This may occur for two reasons. The first is that the player gets so tense and scared on the golf course that she mentally inhibits her performance; or second, the player does not practice in a way that transfers to on-course play.

In this context, let's say it's the second. If you have trouble playing on the course like you practice, it may be that you need to learn how to practice in a way that transfers best to what you encounter on the golf course (assuming that you don't become tense or try too hard on the golf course). The more you can imitate the situations you encounter on the golf course in your practice, the better your chances of playing to your potential.

> **Instead of just hitting balls, make believe every ball represents a shot during the round. Actually visualize the course conditions—where the pin is cut, where the bunkers are, how the match stands.**
> *Nancy Lopez (1987), LPGA Tour*

What usually happens on the golf course? Each shot and putt you play is played in a different set of elements or conditions. Each time you hit a shot, you use a different club, the ball rests differently each time, and the terrain and thickness of the grass are unique. You hit shots from downhill, sidehill, and uphill lies. You hit shots from flyer lies, perched lies, and tight lies. The elements of wind, moisture, and temperature change for each shot. The distance to the target and placement of the target varies on each shot. No two shots are the same, unless you hit a ball out-of-bounds and have to replay the shot.

Practice in a way that helps you perform in real situations on the course.

Putting is very similar in this respect. No two putts are the same. For each putt you hit, the distance, speed, terrain, and grain of the grass is different. This is one reason why golf is such an interesting and challenging game. No two shots are hit in the same conditions.

What do amateur players do on the practice tee? Usually a player hits 30 balls in a row with one club, uses the same target, hits from the same lie and terrain, and hits the same type of shot. This never happens on the golf course, so why do golfers practice this way? Most players would say that they're grooving their swing, and gaining confidence by repeating a movement. Research has shown repeatedly that this type of practice is very effective for getting immediate results in practice but is not effective for long-term learning or transferring what you learned to the course.

Practice rule #1. The first practice rule is to vary your practice and the type of shots you hit. Vary the club that you hit often. Unless you are working strictly on changing your mechanics, don't hit more than two consecutive shots with the same club. Pick out a different target on each shot. Experiment with picking different targets in the distance and changing the targets you select in the range. Changing your target often helps you to set up differently each for each shot, otherwise you begin to dig your feet into a rut and never work on your set-up and alignment.

Golf is a target game: you aim for the fairway; then you aim for the green; then you aim for the cup. Yet all too often amateurs hit ball after ball off the practice tee without aiming at anything specific.

Curtis Strange (1990), PGA Tour

Practicing from various lies improves learning and on-course play.

See what type of target you respond to best. Some players use a tree in the far distance, others use the pin, and some players use an intermediate target two or three feet in front of the ball in line with a distant target. Do you feel more comfortable hitting to a target in the distance or a target closer to you? Change the lie of the ball. Hit uphill, downhill, sidehill shots. Hit shots out of the rough and sand.

Practice hitting different shots by varying your swing. Hit a full shot, a three-quarter shot, a punch shot. Practice drawing and fading the ball with high and low trajectories. The more you can vary the conditions of the shot and the type of shot in practice, the more your practice will transfer to on-course play where you will encounter these situations.

> **Practicing out of divots, off hilly or perched lies, off leaves and pine needles, under and over trees, off moist and dry turf, and all other goofy situations you invariably encounter in golf, prepares you for both the expected and the unexpected.**
> *Seve Ballesteros (1988), PGA Tour*

Practice rule #2. The second practice rule is to simulate on-course play. You can do this by pretending you're playing the course when you are practicing on the range. Hit a driver to a defined target similar to a fairway. Pull out a seven-iron and hit that to a target with borders the size of a green. Use you normal preshot routine when hitting a shot. You use a routine on the course, why not hit shots in practice with your routine? Practice picking targets, seeing the ball fly to the target, and practice your set-up and alignment on each shot.

To increase the difficulty of simulation practice, play mind games with yourself. Imagine a lake in front of you and you have to hit over that lake to a small green. Designate areas in the range that signify the boundaries of the fairway and see how many drives you can get in the fairway. Try hitting shots with imaginary water to the right and out-of-bounds to the left.

Practice rule #3. Vary your putting practice. It's good practice to hit 50 five-foot putts in a row if you are working on putting technique or trying to groove a repeatable swing. But this type of practice does little for developing feel or touch on the greens and maximizing transfer. Feel is the most important element in putting. Every putt you encounter on the golf course is different. Each putt has a different distance, break, speed, and visible look to it.

Use practice time to imagine situations that might be encountered on the course.

One way to develop your feel is repeatedly change the length of putt you hit. Here's a simple drill you can use to help you learn to judge your distances better. Line a few tees up in the ground about two feet apart starting at 10 feet. Place the first tee at 10 feet, the second at 12 feet, the third at 14, and up to 20 feet. Your goal is to hit consecutive putts between the first and second tee, the second and third tee, and all the way up to two feet past the last tee and then back again. If you miss a putt, you must start over. Do this drill putting uphill, downhill, and on a flat surface. You can be creative by change the intervals between the tees and change the length of the putts, depending on a particular "problem distance" you are having trouble judging.

You also must learn to judge how much a putt is going to break. This requires that you hit a variety of putts that break left to right and right to left from several different slopes with various inclines. Here's another drill. Place four tees three feet on each side of a hole that is on a downhill slope. Place three balls on one tee three feet below the hole, three feet above the hole, three feet right of the hole, and three feet left of the hole. Your task is to make all 12 putts consecutively, alternating around the hole hitting from a different position each time. You can increase or decrease the difficulty of this drill by moving the balls further or closer to the hole.

Practice rule #4. Practice rule four is to vary the different drills you do in practice. The research on practice schedules shows that learning occurs faster when you do different drills in one practice session rather than practicing one drill for the entire period. How do you practice? Do you work on one drill for the entire day's session and then work on another part of your game the next session?

---

*Practice different
parts of your game in one
session to maximize learning.*

The most effective use of time would be to alternate the drills and work on different parts of your game in one practice session. Instead of practicing only short irons in one session, vary your routine by practicing all parts of your game; divide your time up and work on putting, chipping, sand play, and long and short irons. This means devoting less time to a given area in one day, but it pays off later because this type of practice enhances long-term learning.

Practice rule #5. Use your normal preshot routine often when practicing both full shots and putting. The only way to get comfortable with your preshot routine is to practice it (refer to Chapter 7 on developing a preshot routine). When you get on the course, you don't want to struggle with trying to recall your preshot routine.

133

Again, making your practice specific to what you do on the course helps to transfer your practice to on-course situations. You can practice your preshot routine anywhere (home, office, golf course) because you don't have to actually hit balls.

Work on Weaknesses as Well as Your Strengths

Many good players make the mistake of practicing more on their strengths than their weaknesses. If the best part of your game is driving the ball, you probably spend more time hitting drivers because you get good results in practice, and therefore enjoy it most. Many golfers shy away from working on weaker parts of their game because they think that they (1) cannot improve that part of their game; (2) are reluctant to practice that part of the game for the fear of "practicing bad habits"; or (3) it's not as interesting or enjoyable to practice when the results are not apparent.

You have to begin by honestly evaluating your game. One way is to rate each of the separate parts of your game after a round. While not perfect, statistics are an objective measure of your strengths and weaknesses. The number of fairways hit estimates your driving accuracy. How many greens you hit in regulation helps to measures your accuracy with irons. Total number of putts per round and average number of putts per green in regulation gives you an idea of putting efficiency. The percentage of sand saves tells you how good you are doing with green-side bunker shots and putting combined. After you chart three or four rounds, you have a good idea of the parts of your game that are stronger and those that are weaker. A player usually can tell, however, which parts of her game are the weakest, even without keeping statistics.

> **I suppose it's just human nature, but we all have a tendency to practice the things we already do pretty well. In truth, we should do just the opposite if we hope to improve.**
> *Nancy Lopez (1987), LPGA Tour*

You must measure your strengths and weaknesses in relation to your level of skill and by comparing the parts of your game. Look at how well you are doing in each part compared to the other parts. If you are hitting 60 percent of fairways off the tee and hitting only 30 percent greens in regulation, that's a good indication that your irons need work. If you are hitting 60 percent of greens in regulation and have 40 total putts per round, this tells you that you need to work on putting.

Make a list of each part of your game from weakest to strongest. Then divide your practice time, spending more time with the areas that need the most work. For example, say your putting needs the greatest improvement, followed by short irons, and then driver. Spend one half your total practice time on putting and the remainder on short irons and driver.

PRACTICE GOOD HABITS, DON'T INGRAIN BAD HABITS

Practicing poor technique is one of the biggest errors made by high-handicapped golfers. Practicing poor mechanics causes you to ingrain bad habits. The more you practice the wrong mechanics, the harder it is to change those poor habits and replace them with fundamentally correct ones. This problem is the most serious for beginning golfers or intermediate players who are improving their swing. The legendary Ben Hogan, one of the greatest golfers of all time, knew that practicing bad habits was one of the most harmful things in golf:

> **It really cuts me up to watch some golfer sweating over his shots on the practice tee, throwing away his energy to no constructive purpose, nine times out of ten doing the say thing wrong he did years and years back when he first took up golf... If he stands out there on the practice tee till he's 90, he's not going to improve. He's going to get worse and worse because he's going to get his bad habits more and more deeply ingrained. (Ben Hogan, 1957)**

This is why instruction at the early state in learning is so important. The more you practice the wrong technique, the harder it is to change and replace the bad habits with correct technique. This is why it is important to know the fundamentals of a good golf swing and use an instructor, teacher, friend, or someone who can look at your swing to see if you are working on correct technique. This can be done by simply asking a knowledgeable player to look at your swing in light of the aspects you are trying to improve. Another way to tell whether you're at least working on the right things is to periodically videotape your swing and then compare your swing to a "model swing," which fits your physical stature and your preferred tempo and swing pattern.

The more you practice the wrong technique, the harder it is to change and adopt good technique.

PRACTICE YOUR MENTAL SKILLS

A good time to develop your mental skills is when you practice the physical parts of your game. You shouldn't wait until you get on the golf course to learn a preshot routine. Spend time on the practice tee developing and ingraining a routine. You don't want to struggle with your routine when it is time to play. Work on developing the specific parts of your routine on the range and practice green.

Practice enhancing your imagery. The practice range is an excellent place to develop the specific parts of your preshot routine. For example, imagery or seeing in your mind's eye is a skill that improves with practice, just as physical skills do. Use this time to improve your imagery and practice getting a picture of the ball flying to the target and feeling a "perfect" shot in your mind. Your main goal while practicing imagery is to increase the vividness and detail of the image of your shot flying to the target. Make the image as life-like and as real as possible. The more vivid you can make the image, the more powerful the image is.

The second goal is to gain total control over the images you project in your mind's eye. Are there times when you get set-up for a shot and see the ball flying into the water? Controlling the image in your mind means seeing the result that you want rather than one you don't want to happen. Practicing your imagery is the best way to increase the control of your images. Begin with a simple task that you have confidence with and then progress to more difficult ones with which you are not as confident.

You also can practice your feel for a good swing or a solidly hit shot. Different types of shots that you might play such as a high shot, draw, fade, and punch, each have a specific feeling for you. A punch shot has a different feeling than a full shot because you don't take a full backswing or a full follow-through. Ingrain a clear kinesthetic feeling for each of the shots you play and practice.

Practice your mental skills during physical practice.

Practice your tension control. Even though you don't become beset by anxiety or pressure on the practice tee, this is a good place to develop your tension control techniques. First, you must decide what tension control method works best for you, and at what stage of your routine you will use it. The use of breathing and tightening and

137

release are two simple, physical ways of reducing excess tension. I suggest using breath control at the start of your preshot routine to clear your mind and help get a sharper image of the shot you want to hit.

In other sports, athletes usually take a deep breath in the beginning of their routine; the basketball player before a foul shot, a pitcher before the pitch, a batter before setting-up in the batter's box, and a placekicker before the snap. You can also take a deep breath in the final stages of your routine as a final check for excess tension. I have even instructed some golfers to take a breath while they are stroking a putt! You can use your breathing at any point, but the first and last stages of your routine are often effective times to employ it.

Tightening and releasing your muscles is also beneficial for reducing excess tension. This can be done at different stages in your preshot preparation. You can tighten and release when you take a breath at the start of the routine by simply tightening your arms and shoulders (shoulder shrug) as you inhale and then releasing the contraction as you exhale. Sometime when playing, you begin to grip the club too tightly without noticing it. Some players choose to tighten the muscles in their hands and arms as they grip the club and then release the contraction to make sure their grip pressure is correct. Practice your tension control methods on the practice tee by contracting and releasing your muscles and working on your breathing.

Other methods of tension control are also effective for use in your routine. One is self-talk or what you say to yourself. An excellent method to help control tension and instill confidence is self-affirmation statements. Affirmations are rehearsed statements that you say to yourself during your preshot routine, or any other time. Phrases such as "you've practiced this shot many times, now just do it," "you're the best at this type of shot," or "my swing feels strong and smooth" are examples of affirmations you make to yourself. Greg Norman uses self-talk right before he hits a tough shot or as encouragement:

> **The tougher the shot I'm facing, the more I talk [to myself]. If I'm on the last hole of a tournament, facing a long iron shot to the green and needing a birdie to win, I'll say to myself, "You know this shot cold, you've knocked it stiff a thousand times, and now you're going to do it again." (Norman & Peper, 1993)**

You can use affirmations or positive self-talk at any point in your routine if they don't interfere with other parts of your routine. You must take time in practice to develop affirmations that are effective for you.

Practice trusting your swing. Learning to trust your swing, which was discussed in Chapter 4, is very important in achieving peak performance, but it is also a skill that must be practiced. There are several drills you can practice and methods you can use in your routine to help increase trust. One way of practicing trust is to shut off your analytical, judgmental mind, which likes to work on technique. Instead, practice focusing on a target and reacting to the target. This takes discipline for the golfer who feels like she always has to be working on technique when practicing.

---

*Use drills in practice
to increase your
trust on the course.*

Another way to practice trust is to develop a swing key that helps to free you when swinging. A swing key is a thought or a feeling you use just prior to the pulling the trigger that helps you focus on a certain aspect of your performance. Technical swing thoughts make you think about the mechanics of your swing, which decreases your ability to trust what you have learned. Rather than thinking about how to do it, pick a swing key that helps you to let it rip and just do it. "Just look and go," "let it rip," "give up control," or "smooth tempo" are examples of swing cues that help you to free your mind and trust your swing.

You can be creative and develop drills that foster trust. Try hitting balls on a tee with your eyes closed. Try to just tune into the feeling of your swing without controlling it. Try taking a couple of practice swings next to the ball focusing on the tempo of your swing and then step up and hit the ball with the same tempo. The key is to find a drill that is the most effective for allowing you to increase your trust on the course.

139

Practice your focusing skills. Concentration is a key ingredient in playing to your potential. The ability to concentrate is also a learned skill. Pros have learned by experience that focusing their attention on the task is critical to optimal performance or they would not be pros. A good time to work on your focusing skills is when you practice on the range or practice green. Narrow your attention to what you're trying to improve in your swing or practice shifting your focus from external (a target) to internal (a swing cue).

Focused practice takes effort and intense concentration. When you practice for a long period of time do you start to lose your concentration? Concentration involves attending to what you want to and doing so for extended periods of time. When you become fatigued on the practice range, your concentration may slip. When concentration begins to slip, this is the time to refocus and become more immersed in your practice. If you are unable to refocus and start concentrating, then it is time to go home, knowing you can start fresh the next time.

DEVELOP A PREROUND PRACTICE ROUTINE

The way you prepare your mind and body before a tournament round is a very important part of achieving peak performance. Most tour pros have a specific preround routine they follow from the time they wake until they tee off. Usually, a pro plans on being at the golf course about one hour prior before tee time and even earlier if she eats at the golf course.

The player has a specific practice routine she follows prior to teeing off. Amy Alcott, winner of 32 professional tournaments including four majors, describes her preround practice: she gets to the golf course about 45 minutes before tee time and begins by stretching her muscles, then she warms-up by hitting a few soft wedge shots, visualizing each shot she hits. Skipping every other club, she works up to her driver, not moving to the next club until she hits the previous club solidly. She finishes the session by hitting a few more soft wedge shots to help her tempo and touch before she starts. Finally, she goes to the practice green and hits a few putts and chips to develop her sense of touch.

All players are different in how they prepare for a tournament round, but they all have a systematic routine. They have learned a system that is best suited to prepare mentally and physically for the day's round. The key is to allow yourself enough time to do your normal practice routine without hurrying. Rushing to the course, warming-up fast, and running to the first tee usually pulls you out of your normal rhythm and makes you anxious before you even begin.

Practice routine for shots. If you don't have a set routine, I would suggest that you warm-up using the clubs you feel most comfortable or confident hitting. If you like hitting the seven-iron better than the six, then use it. Start with a club that is easier to hit such as a wedge or short iron and progress to the longer clubs. Don't finish the session by hitting full-force drivers. Finish your session by hitting one-half shots using a short iron. This will help you to regain a smooth tempo prior to teeing off. Ending warm-up with the driver sometimes causes an increase your tempo and makes you want to "kill" the ball on the golf course.

Kelly Gibson, winner of the 1991 Manitoba Open and nominated for PGA Tour Rookie of the Year in 1992, must make sure he maintains his tempo during preround practice. Kelly, fourth in driving distance on the tour in 1992, is a main attraction during preround practice. When he hits his driver in practice, the fans "oooh and aaah" at the distance he attains. In the past, this spurred him to impress the crowd and try to hit the ball further and further, taking him out of his normal rhythm. When he went from the practice tee to the first tee, his pace was causing him to overswing on the course. Kelly has learned to hit only three or four drivers with good tempo during his warm-up, and wind down his swing by hitting a few lazy sand wedges.

You also don't want to hit too many balls during your preround practice because you don't want to drain your energy for the day.

Practice routine for the short game. The most important preround preparation on the putting green is developing a feel for the speed of the greens and getting some positive feedback. Hit several putts from a variety of longer distances to help you gauge the speed of the green. Next, you may want to hit some short putts around the hole from below, above, and the sides of a cup that is on a slope to help develop your feel for how much the ball breaks on the green. Lastly, hit some putts within your comfort zone, say from two to four feet, to get a positive image of the ball rolling into the hole.

141

It's also important to hit a few shots from the bunker to test the sand and how the ball flies from the bunker. It is good to know before you get on the course if you need to adjust your swing based on the firmness and texture of the sand. Getting a feel for chip shots is also important. You might hit a few chips from different lies around the green. This helps you gauge how the ball will come out of the rough and gives you an idea of the firmness of the green and the amount of role you can expect.

Warm-up is only a warm-up. Keep in mind that a warm-up is just a warm-up. You don't have to win warm-ups. This is a time to loosen your muscles, get a feel for your swing, and prepare your mind for play. If you worry because you're not hitting the ball well in practice, then you set yourself up for failure. John Daly isn't concerned with how well he hits the ball on the range during warm-ups. If he hits it badly in warm-ups, he doesn't feel it is relevant to how he plays in the tournament. He understands that the purpose of preround practice is to get a feeling for his swing and to get loose. He knows that the practice range is a wide open area, which is totally different than what is encountered on the golf course.

> *Preround practice is for getting loose and preparing the body for what's to follow.*

Many players hit the ball poorly in warm-ups, but hit it well on the course. These players don't concentrate well on the practice range because there are no defined holes and targets to which to hit. Also, these players need additional stimulus to help them focus better. When they get on the course, their concentration improves because of the excitement of the event or because they know that they are about to play when it "means" something. The opposite can also happen. Some players hit the ball fine on the range, but freeze and overcontrol their swing on the golf course.

CHAPTER SUMMARY

•   Quality practice involves giving your complete attention to what you are doing and practicing in a way that best transfers to situations that you encounter on the golf course.

•   When you practice, have a specific idea of what you are working on. Think about one aspect of your swing at a time and then move on to the next area to be improved.

•   Set both performance and outcome goals for each practice session. Use mini-goals to achieve your long-term objectives. Goals should be specific, measurable, and revised often to match your level of play.

•   The best type of practice is practice that matches what you will do and encounter on the golf course. Vary your practice often including the lie of the ball, the type of shot, and the club you use to hit each shot. Vary your putting practice by hitting putts with different distances and breaks.

•   Work on the weak parts of your game just as much as the strong parts. Don't ingrain bad habits by practicing improper technique. Find an instructor you can work with so you are practicing good habits.

•   Practice your mental skills during physical practice. Work on improving your imagery skills, tension control, focusing and trusting skills.

•   Develop a preround practice routine that will increase the consistency of your mental and physical preparation for a round. Get a sense for how your swing feels, how fast the greens are and how far your chips roll on the green. Don't get caught up in worrying about having a good preround practice session, it is only a warm-up. Many players play better when they get on the golf course.

9

SPECIAL CHALLENGES IN GOLF:

COMFORT ZONES, PATIENCE, ENJOYING GOLF, AND COMMITMENT AND MOTIVATION

The saying that golf is 90 percent mental applies here, meaning that not only do you have to think your way around the course, but you have to keep a handle on your emotions so that they don't interfere with your ability to make smart decisions. That can be difficult, since there's so much downtime in golf, giving you plenty of opportunity to scold yourself for hitting a horrible shot as you search for your ball in the woods or berate yourself for missing that three-footer...
Curtis Strange (1990), PGA Tour

Golf, like other sports, has particular challenges that players must overcome to play to their potential. The nature of golf requires the mental toughness and ability to overcome frustration, impatience, and perfectionistic tendencies. Chapter 9 discusses the unique psychological demands in golf, including comfort zones, being patient, and how players stop having fun in a game that was intended to be played for fun. In golf, you are your own coach, trainer, and sport psychologist, and ultimately, you must decide what is best.

THE DEMANDS OF GOLF

A unique feature of golf is the abundant amount of time you have to think on the golf course. Most sports require the participant to be actively engaged for most of the game. In many team sports, there is less free time to think and more time is spent reacting to a ball and/or other players. In golf, there is abundant downtime between shots (and while you wait for others to play) when you are not actively engaged in play. The ball stands still until you are ready to propel it. How you choose to deal with the downtime can influence your performance. The extra downtime makes some players become too analytical and judgmental between shots.

For golfers, golf is the ultimate individual sport. Although you play with others, you are alone on the golf course. You have no teammates to help you or on whom to rely. When you play well, you take all the credit for your success. When you play poorly, you must also take the blame for your failure. You cannot blend into the crowd or blame another person when you slice a ball out-of-bounds, or when you miss a three-foot putt to lose the match.

When you learn the fundamentals of the game, your mental approach to golf is the key to unlocking your physical potential. Most players I know when they don't play well go back to the drawing board and put in more effort to improve their game. The problem is that most players don't understand whether they lost because of a physical error or poor thought processes. It is easy to correct a problem with some work on the range, but it's not that simple if the problem was caused by a mental error. Players aren't sure how to correct a mental error because most do not understand how the mind works.

> **You can hit a great shot and end up 10 or 15 feet from the hole, or you can hit a lousy shot and it goes in the hole, and that's just the nature of golf.**
> *David Edwards, PGA Tour*

The nature of the game is paradoxical. Hitting a ball that is two-and-a-half inches in diameter with a 43-inch-long club with a clubhead four inches wide that is traveling at 120 mph into a cup that is four inches in diameter is an imperfect task. Yet, the challenge of this task keeps golfers coming back for more. What is even more astonishing is that the nature of the game breeds perfectionism. To be successful in golf requires physical talent, intense practice, mental fortitude, and a level of commitment and motivation that approaches perfectionism. The irony is that golf is an imperfect game that produces perfectionists. The more you play and the better you get, the more you expect to play flawlessly in a game that cannot be played to perfection.

Golf is a game that never can be perfected, but yet it fosters perfectionism.

THE MYSTERY OF THE COMFORT ZONE

When I work with golfers one of the biggest challenges is overcoming "comfort zones" or scoring zones. A comfort zone is an expectation a player has about his ability to shoot a certain score. A comfort zone, or what would more appropriately be called a "discomfort zone," is a feeling of discomfort when you play outside of your normal scoring zone.

Most players expect they can shoot within a certain scoring range on a given day. John, for example, usually shoots in the mid-80s and has a scoring zone of plus or minus five shots from his average score. On a good day he shoots 79, on a bad day he shoots 90. In the back of his mind he knows what he can usually shoot. He always manages to play within his comfort zone because of the expectations he holds. If he shoots 37 on the front nine, he may think I've never shot better than 76, and then he proceeds to shoot 43 on the back nine. Conversely, if he shoots 46 on the front nine, he says I'm too good a player to shoot 90, and he plays himself back into his comfort zone and shoots 39 on the back nine.

We limit ourselves with expectations that we set for ourselves.

Players at all levels seem to be afflicted with a comfort zone. A professional is out of his comfort zone when he is one or two over par on an easy course. A high handicap golfer, who is playing well, feels awkward when playing better than he expects. When your expectations don't match your play, you consciously or unconsciously find a way to play back to your comfort zone. A comfort zone is similar to a self-fulfilling prophesy, which occurs when what you believe will happen actually does happen because of your expectations.

Maintain your aggressive style. How does a player not handicap himself with a comfort zone? A comfort zone is a problem for a golfer who plays above his expectations and then self-sabotages his play later in the round. It starts when you lose your focus and become score-conscious. You notice you are playing better that expected and then unconsciously undermine your play. You may change your game plan and try to protect the score that you could shoot if you "don't screw it up."

Instead of firing at the pin and aggressively rolling putts past the hole, you suddenly turn defensive to protect your lead. This style of play seeks to avoid failure, rather than going aggressively after the best round of your life. You notice the trouble areas more and begin to worry about the consequences of bad shots. Soon, your defensive style of play causes you to hit the ball fat or leave birdie putts five feet short when you haven't done either all day. A good example of this is when a tour pro squanders a four-shot lead the last nine holes of a tournament because he tried to safeguard his lead. You have to maintain the same style of play that got you in position to shoot a good score, rather than adopting a cautious style of play in order to maintain your lead.

"Don't mess-up a good round, just shoot for the middle of the green"

Trying to protect your score often causes you to become too defensive and cautious, which can lead to poor play.

You must think about continuing to play boldly. If you are playing well, what is stopping you from continuing to play well? You are! This is the time when you should play boldly and aggressively. How many chances do you get to play confidently and feel like you can't do anything wrong? Stay with your game plan and don't accept the attitude that you must safeguard your score.

You only get what you expect. On the golf course, you have to learn to discard your expectations. Humans are the only beings that place limits on their potential. You must start the day having confidence and believing you have the ability to par or birdie every hole on the golf course. But don't expect to birdie every hole. When you start to play "above" your expectation, assume that you are only playing near your maximum potential. I don't believe in the concept of playing above your ability. How can a person play above their physical and mental ability? For once, you are playing to your potential.

Stay focused in the present. A player who projects the score she will shoot and then questions if that score matches her expectations for herself is not focused on playing one shot at a time. She is thinking ahead about a finishing score and not focusing on the task, which is to get the ball into the hole in the least number of strokes. The problem starts when the player realizes that she is playing better than expected, which causes her to think about holes still to come.

This is the time when you should refocus your mind on the process of hitting good shots. Without a process, present-oriented focus, you are doomed to think about a final score and the consequences of each shot before you even hit the shot (refer to Chapter 6 on immersing yourself in the shot).

PATIENCE

Golf presents several unique challenges to players of all levels, but a major one of these is the struggle against impatience. The two types of patience that I deal with most often are on-course patience and patience for improving your game. I have seen many players turn an average round into a rotten round because they lost their patience after a bad break or an error. Lipping-out three birdie putts in a row, playing well and then having one shot spoil a good round, and playing conservatively but hitting the ball into a bad position are examples of situations that cause players to become frustrated, take more gambles, and try too hard on the golf course.

Impatience makes things worse because you start to press, gamble more, and try too hard.

The problem with losing patience is that it causes you to change your game plan and sometimes be too aggressive or try too hard. The player who missed three easy birdie putts thinks that he has to hit the ball closer to make a birdie. He begins to force it and play more aggressively, trying to hit everything close to the pin. This approach often backfires, making a player more frustrated, try even harder, and be even more aggressive. During Amy Alcott's third year on tour, she became impatient after losing a few tournaments she thought she should have won. She put so much pressure on herself that she began to lose her patience, which caused her to gamble more:

> I was consumed with the idea of winning and I was trying everything I could think of to force a win. I was practicing more than I needed to, which was making my game stale. I was taking gambles on the golf course that weren't necessary. I was grinding over every shot. And the more I did this the more frustrated I became. (Amy Alcott, 1990)

On-course composure. It is easy to tell someone to be more patient, but what does it mean? Patience means maintaining your composure and sticking with your game plan. It means not becoming frustrated when you play conservatively and it doesn't pay off, and then forcing every shot. It means not losing your poise when you lip-out four times in a row and then start to charge every putt. Patience means not letting taxing situations hinder your ability to make good decision on the golf course. I think the best solution is to understand that losing composure over something that is in the past causes you to make poor decisions at hand as well as future shots. If you lipped-out, it is in the past. Why carry the frustration caused by

150

the last shot to your next shot? It not only ruins your state of mind but also causes you to focus on the past rather than your present shot.

Off-course patience. Impatience is also a problem with players who are intolerant of not improving their game fast enough. As you improve your skills in golf, it is harder to see measurable improvements in your game. You reach a ceiling or a plateau where an increase in practice doesn't lead to measurable improvements. This is the point where impatience and frustration begins.

It becomes discouraging when you practice a lot and don't see the improvements in your game you've expected. When you spend a lot of time working on your game it doesn't always pay off immediately. Often, when you make a big change, your play gets worse before it gets better.

Think about the last time you had a lesson. You made a swing change that felt awful and it produced poor results, but you stayed with it because you had confidence in your instructor. You didn't see immediate improvements and you actually played poorly while you worked on the change. After ingraining the change in memory, you began to improve and started to play better. Don't become frustrated if you cannot see instant improvements in your game. Eventually, with the proper technique and quality practice, your work will pay off. Remember that less skilled players always have greater rates of improvement than higher skilled players.

CHOOSING TO HAVE FUN

Another unique challenge is having fun on the golf course. This problem occurs in all sports, but the particular demands of golf sometimes make it difficult to enjoy yourself. I impress on players that the game is supposed to be played for fun, regardless of whether or not golf is a career. Somewhere along the way it becomes more serious and players lose the enjoyment of the game.

Golf is an imperfect game played by people who are trying to perfect their game but who can never reach perfection. The game can be very frustrating for golfers at all levels. A three-foot putt can turn into a life or death situation if the game is not kept in perspective. These inherent frustrations of the game sometimes make it hard to fully enjoy the game. Expecting perfection is irrational because humans do make errors and you are human. The next time you make an error and become frustrated remember that golf is an imperfect game played by people who are prone to make mistakes.

> **If you aren't trying to earn a living by playing golf, believe me it isn't worth getting that steamed up. Remember that golf is a game meant for recreation.**
> *Curtis Strange (1990), PGA Tour*

Golf requires a great amount of practice and play if one is to improve and become successful. This predisposes golfers to become stale or suffer burnout. Any task that is done repeatedly can cause a person to lose interest or become bored, if they don't find ways to make it enjoyable. Intense amounts of practice or playing day after day can cause you to become physically tired to the point of feeling lethargic, and it is no fun to play in that state. Also, if you are physically tired, then their is a good chance that you will be mentally tired, which causes you to be lazy with your psychological skills on the golf course.

If you have trouble staying fresh and enjoying the game, think about what tour pros must endure. They play as many as 45 weeks a year, six days a week, and as much as eight hours a day. During a typical day, a tour pro may practice for an hour before he plays, play for four to five hours, and then practice another hour or two after the round. If anyone is susceptible to burnout, it's the tour pro.

What do you enjoy about the game? Regardless of the reasons that caused you to stop having fun, the first suggestion is to remember why you enjoy playing. Do you like the physical activity? Do you enjoy golf because you enjoy striking a ball properly and the feeling that brings? Do you play to socialize and be with other people? Do you enjoy being in the outdoors? Examine the reasons why you enjoy the game. When you first started to play, what was fun about the game? The next time you feel frustrated, angry, tired, or stale, remember why you enjoy playing.

Accept that everyone makes mistakes. As I said earlier, golf is an imperfect game played by imperfect humans. Players who expect perfection are doomed before they begin. I'm amazed when I see a player who is playing well hit one bad shot and then fall apart.

This player is so consumed with thinking about how mad he is for hitting one bad shot that all the other good shots he hit are forgotten.

Golf is a humbling game. You have to accept that you are human, and humans are not perfect and will make mistakes. Everyone has bad days, even the pros. When you played your best round, did you make any mistakes? Probably so, but it was easier to forget them. The best players in the world when they are on the top of their game make mistakes just like everyone else. Great players learn to accept that they hit bad shots and putts occasionally. They have learned to go on and stay focused on the task, rather than let their emotions spoil the rest of the round.

Enjoy the moment. At some point golf loses its playfulness and becomes a serious game for most golfers. When golf becomes too serious, the fun vanishes from the game, because it is no longer just a game. Instead of having fun, your goal is to beat your opponent, impress a friend, or shoot your lowest score. When you become too serious on the golf course you have to rearrange your priorities. The old saying that you must "stop and smell the roses" applies here. Sometimes it helps to settle for enjoying the surroundings and your company. Most golf courses are on the most beautiful pieces of land in the country.

Research on flow and motivation reveals that people gain enjoyment from just participating in the activity for itself. An activity can be enjoyed for the pure sake of playing and does not need to be dependent on rewards, recognition, or praise from others. If you enjoy golf primarily because you like rewards or prizes, praise from others, or monetary gains, and you don't receive these, your level of enjoyment fluctuates depending on how many external rewards you receive.

> **The act of winning is satisfying, but it's the fight and the battle that you go through that's the fun part.**
> *Bob Tway, PGA Tour*

Flow occurs when a person becomes immersed in a challenging activity that matches the person's skills. Enjoyment occurs when a person's mind becomes "lost" in an activity and the person receives feedback about how he is doing. Golf provides both of these elements. When concentration is fully devoted to the task at hand, there is no room left in your consciousness to concern yourself with problems at the office, school, or at home.

It is difficult to reach a state of flow when you are either bored or anxious. Feeling bored usually results from feeling a lack of challenge from the task. You may become bored when you play an opponent who is not as good as you, or you play a course that is not challenging enough for you. Anxiety or fear, on the other hand, result from your perception of the task being too hard for your skill level. This occurs when you play someone who is better than you, or you have to hit a shot that is above your skill level.

*It is harder to become
immersed in an activity
that presents too small
or too big of a challenge.*

In either case, a challenge that is too high or too low makes it harder for you to get into the flow and enjoy the activity. Thus, you have to find a way of matching your present skill level with a task that is challenging but not too difficult. This may require you to arrange your goals to match your skill level. For example, instead of playing to win a match in which your opponent is much better than you, you might set a goal to hit a certain percentage of fairways and greens. On the other hand, if you're bored, you may have to create a challenge that will help you become immersed in the game.

It's fun to see improvements. Golf requires a great amount of self-determination to continue to improve, especially at the higher levels where improvements are difficult to see and only come with greater effort. Even amateurs must be self-motivated and very persistent to improve their game. Striving to better your game can be a major source of enjoyment. Achieving your goals and seeing improvements in your game can give you a sense of accomplishment and self-determination. That's why setting mini-goals for yourself is important. Reaching your short-term goals allow you to see small improvements in your performance.

MOTIVATION AND COMMITMENT

A key ingredient to achieving peak performance is maintaining the proper level of motivation. Everyone is motivated differently and brings a certain level of motivation to their sport or career. Motivation falls under a continuum from too low to too high. In some cases, players lack motivation and don't work to be the best they can be. Other players have too much motivation, which causes them to work so hard that they become stale and unproductive. In this section, I discuss the problems of lack of motivation and overmotivation, and give you strategies for achieving a level of motivation that is most productive for you.

DO YOU HAVE A HEALTHY LEVEL OF MOTIVATION?

You hear athletes in all sports attribute their success to dedication and hard work. There is no doubt that motivation is a key ingredient to success in any sport. The best coaches in history have been excellent motivators. In golf, you don't have a coach who constantly motivates you to practice hard and play your best. Your level of motivation is determined by how you choose to motivate yourself.

> **The people who excel are those who are driven to show the world—and prove to themselves—just how good they are.**
> *Nancy Lopez (1987), LPGA Tour*

Motivation is divided into two elements: the intensity and direction of behavior. The intensity of motivation refers to how activated you are or how much effort you give to attain your goals. The direction of motivation refers to the goals you have for yourself or what you want to achieve with your game. An increase in either intensity or direction, increases your level of motivation.

Motivation can also be divided into two general sources of motivation: intrinsic and extrinsic motivation. Intrinsically motivated athletes are motivated for personal reasons including mastering a task, feeling competent, having fun, and being self-determined. Extrinsically motivated athletes are motivated by external rewards like money, public recognition, or praise from others. Most athletes are motivated by both extrinsic and intrinsic reasons.

Qualities of undermotivated golfers. Golfers who lack motivation either do not apply themselves with the needed effort or do not have a clear vision of their goals. There are several reasons, too numerous to cover here, why golfers lack motivation. In an extreme case, a person who lacks motivation has learned early in his life that he doesn't need to work as hard as others to be successful. This person may have experienced a good deal of success early in life leading him to conclude that he is a "natural" player. He also feels that he always performs well in sport regardless of the amount of effort given, which drains later effort.

This athlete usually develops a high level of confidence in his ability and makes him feel that his success is a result of his natural talent. This feeling leads to overconfidence where the player learns that effort and persistence are not very important to his success. By not placing emphasis on persistence and hard work, the player lacks healthy work habits to be the best he can be. Practice is a waste of time for this player because he thinks it won't have an influence on the outcome of the match. Others players label this player as lazy and indifferent. His confidence in his ability helps him perform well in competition, but he lacks the work ethic to be the best he can be.

Fred Couples was stereotyped by his fellow players earlier in his career as a player with immense talent but lacking motivation. He was criticized by other players because he didn't appear to "care" as much or work as hard as others, yet he played as well as anyone. I am not saying, however, that Fred lacks motivation; he responded harshly when a player criticized his motivation and commitment. Fred said that he wants to play well just as much as the next person, but that he is a person who does not show it on the outside. With a renewed sense of commitment to becoming the best he can be, Fred had the best year of his career in 1992, winning three times and finishing first on the PGA Tour official money list, and was crowned Player of the Year.

Qualities of overmotivated golfers. Persistence, effort, determination, and a strong work ethic are excellent qualities to possess in any endeavor. What most people don't understand is that dedication and persistence can be taken to an extreme, and this can interfere with reaching peak performance. A good work ethic is important, but a player who is too goal-oriented and perfectionistic runs the risk of working so hard that he becomes stale or reaches burnout. This player also runs the risk of being scared and anxious in competition because he or she tries too hard to play well, which leads to overcontrol and being analytical and judgmental on the course.

Trying too hard is often ineffective in golf. Overtrying increases tension and causes you to steer your shot.

Most perfectionistic players have learned early in their lives from others that hard work and effort are the keys to success. A perfectionist sets extremely high goals and goes after those goals with intense levels of effort and persistence. When this person fails or is blocked from attaining these goals, he or she increases effort and determination, thinking that this is the path to success. Soon, this player's determination is so extreme and he or she works so hard and wants to succeed so badly that he or she becomes afraid of failing and still doesn't realize his or her full potential.

*A player who wants to play
well so badly trips himself
because he overworks everything.*

This type of player has trouble playing well in competition because of his intense desire for attaining his goals. Unlike the player
who lacks direction and effort, this player becomes anxious and has
trouble keeping his mind on the present task. An overmotivated
player evaluates and analyzes his play and is very critical of his mistakes, which lead to a need to perfect his mechanics (refer to Chapter
4 on "Learning to Let it Flow"). He is caught in a negative cycle.
When he fails, he becomes frustrated, responds with higher commitment and effort to attain his goals, works harder to achieve his goals,
and tries even harder in competition, which leads to choking or
wanting so badly to play well that he becomes crippled by anxiety.

CHANGING YOUR LEVEL OF MOTIVATION

There are both positive and negative qualities of undermotivated
and overmotivated players. You can balance your level of motivation by learning from both types of players. The ideal player is the
dedicated player combined with the self-confident player who plays
free in competition. Having a strong work ethic and high goals, as
well as persistence and high effort in practice, when coupled with
high self-confidence and belief in your ability, and a present-oriented
focus and good mentality for competition are the best ingredients for
optimal levels of personal motivation. Giving your full effort to prepare the best you can for competition and then being able to trust
yourself and play relaxed in competition is the key to achieving optimal performance.

INCREASING YOUR MOTIVATION

The player who lacks motivation has to start by understanding
that he can improve his game with increased effort and better work
habits. This player thinks that practice and hard work is a waste of

time. This attitude is ineffective and must be changed. An undermotivated player has to start thinking differently about his ability to improve and do some things that he has not done in the past.

Talent and hard work equals success. Physical talent without hard work and dedication is a waste. Success is a product of having physical abilities that allow a player to succeed and a strong work ethic that helps improve a player's physical skills. Physical ability is inborn, but skills are learned and modified through practice and play. You cannot change the ability given to you at birth, but you can improve your physical skills. Bruce Lietzke is an example a player who seems to practice less than others but plays well in tournaments. Many of his fellow players joke about how he can take two weeks off without practice and come back and win the next tournament. Most likely, however, he practiced a great deal early in his career. While he is an exception, he has learned to keep his skills sharp with limited practice.

Focus more on your goals. One problem with an undermotivated player is his lack of direction. One way to gain better practice habits is to set goals. Goals give you a sense of purpose and direction in practice and increase effort and persistence in a task. You can set both competitive goals and practice goals. Competitive goals include things like decreasing your strokes per round, fairways hit per round, greens hit in regulation, and number of putts per round. You can use practice goals to help you reach your competitive goals (refer to Chapter 8 on setting goals in practice).

Increase pride and joy in practice. Players who lack motivation think that practice is too boring or lacking challenge. Finding ways to enjoy practice and make it more challenging is an excellent way to develop better work habits. One way is to play mind games and challenge yourself in practice. Test yourself and see how many balls you can hit to an imagined fairway on the range, or how many greens you can hit in a row. Test your concentration and see how many quality, focused shots you can hit on the range without losing your focus. Challenge yourself by hitting different types of shot, trick shots, and recovery shots.

Increase your excitement by competing with other players in practice. Present a challenge to another player. One way to do this is to play "call your shot" where each player takes turn selecting a certain type of shot (fade, draw, punch, etc.) that the other player has to hit. Select 10 balls and see who can get the most balls closest to the pin or in the fairway. Compete with another player on the practice green. Play 18 holes on the practice green hitting putts with your eyes closed. Put a small wager on the game. Test your skills and see who can chip a ball in first from different positions around the green. Be creative and you will find there are several games you can play to make your practice more enjoyable.

Work on weaknesses. Each golfer has strong and weak parts of her game. To develop better practice habits, you must begin by assessing the areas of your game that are strong and weak, and dedicate yourself to working on the weaker areas. One way to become a better player is to bring the weaker parts of your game up to parity with your strengths.

Dealing With Overmotivation

An overmotivated player has plenty of energy to devote to practicing and working on technique. The challenge for the player with excessive motivation is to stop being so serious and overcontrolled, and play more relaxed and in the present. This player wants to play well so badly that he has trouble focusing in the present. He constantly worries about the consequences and outcomes of his actions. The key for the overmotivated player is to learn to relax, have more fun, and become more present-oriented.

Stay in the present. If you are anxious, tense, or try too hard on the course, the first area that you need to improve upon is staying in the present and focusing on the process of hitting a good shot. Most anxiety and fear is directed toward the future by worrying about what may or may not happen. Under normal situations, you focus on the ingredients of your routine and think about what you need to do to hit your best shot. You get anxious and distracted when your mind becomes filled with thoughts of missing an important putt, hitting a ball over the green, or hitting a ball into the water.

Emphasize fun not winning. The anxiety you experience partially results from an overemphasis on winning and playing well. Everybody is trying to win and play well, so you don't need to have those as your primary goals. Your competitive goal should be to

160

play for fun and the enjoyment of the game. This is easier said than done for golfers who constantly tie themselves up in knots because they try too hard to play well. You have to change you normal way of thinking and condition your mind to focus on the joy you get from play regardless of how you play.

> **Ultimately I play because I love the game and that can be a fantastic motivator.**
> *Trevor Dodds, PGA Tour*

You should learn to be more internally motivated, motivated to play for the pure enjoyment of the game regardless of external rewards, praise, or monetary gains. Research on motivation says that external rewards can hurt your motivation if the rewards are controlling your behavior without providing information about how well you are doing on the course.

Take a time out. Understand that you can work too hard on your game and become stale or suffer burnout. It is analogous to the long distance runner who ran five miles a day and competed well at that level of training. She started to think that seven miles a day would be better, then 10 miles a day, then 15 miles a day. The extra training soon became counterproductive and she was doing more harm than good. When she competes, she cannot give her best because she is physically exhausted, stale, and burned out due to overtraining.

On the PGA Tour, a player sometimes wins a tournament after taking two weeks off without touching a club. A break in action allows you to come back fresh, energetic, and more focused. You don't have to take two weeks off, but relaxing your practice routine or taking a few days off can be beneficial when you return. Taking a few days off helps to refresh your mind and play less mechanically. Learn to recognize when you start to overpractice and spin your wheels, so you can take a time out and come back with a fresh mind and body.

Don't dwell on mistakes. If you are a perfectionist, you spend most of your time dwelling on your mistakes and weaknesses. This is unhealthy for your self-confidence and doesn't let you enjoy golf. Always dwelling on your weaknesses and errors sends a message to yourself that you are never good enough. You are not a failure, you just choose to think more about your faults.

You have to make the choice to think about positive aspects of your game and remember the good shots instead of replaying the bad shots over and over. "If I just would have made those three short putts, I could have played well today" is what a negative player says about his play. He forgets about the five long putts that he made and the numerous other shots that he hit well. Give yourself more credit for your play. Remember the good shots you hit and replay those shots in your mind.

Give yourself permission to make mistakes. Perfectionists think that anything less than a flawless performance is a failure. An 80 should have been 78, an 85 should have been 82. The perfectionist who wins a match but didn't play perfectly views his performance as a failure. Perfectionists have to accept that they are human and they will make mistakes just like everyone else. Also, failure is a statistical probability in this game. You are going to lose much more often than you win in golf, that's simply the nature of the game. When you lose, don't equate that loss with your personal worth. It's simply a game. Don't judge your personal value on the basis of how you play the game.

Sometimes it helps to give yourself permission to make a couple of mistakes in a round. You're not perfect and even the best players in the world make mistakes. Allowing yourself to make an error takes the pressure off yourself. It also allows you to play on after a first error without ruining your game. I am not asking you to expect mistakes; I am saying that you need to accept mistakes when they happen. Golf is a game of misses and of minimizing mistakes; it's not a game to be perfected.

Be patient, give improvements time. A problem for most players, particularly at higher levels, is a lack of patience for improvements in their game. As your skills improve, it is harder to see measurable improvements in your play. You begin to approach a ceiling where smaller and smaller improvements in your skills occur. You become impatient, work harder, and become frustrated because you cannot see gains or you want to see faster gains, even though you still may be improving. Realize that skills progress quickly early in learning. The better you become, the slower your skills improve. Be patient with progress in your game, particularly if your skills are well developed.

Work on your mental game. Players who are extremely motivated usually are very dedicated to working on their physical game and improving technique. Dedication is a positive quality if it is helping you get where you want to go. A dedication to the searching for the perfect swing or overtraining can be counterproductive if you are compulsive about it. You then tend to neglect other important parts of your game, including your mental approach.

> **I got to a point where hard work didn't seem to accomplish a whole lot, I was spinning my wheels... So I backed off on working hard and focused more on the mental part.**
> *David Edwards, PGA Tour*

If you spend most of your time working on perfecting your method, it is time to channel your energy and dedication into working on the mental side of your game. The mental side is the primary area that you must work on for you to reach your potential. You have all that it takes to play your best: ability, skill, motivation, commitment, and dedication, but you haven't been able to realize your full potential. It's time for you to evaluate what holds you back, change your ineffective attitudes and beliefs, and become a mentally tough player.

COMMITMENT AND DEDICATION

The final ingredient to achieving peak performance is commitment. When I speak of commitment, I am referring to two areas. The first is a general commitment to your game and the desire to improve. The second is a commitment to playing your best with the ambition to improve your mental game. You must combine both motivation and commitment to continue your development as a player in order to reach your full potential. One without the other is not a sufficient means for realizing your potential. You can be highly motivated but lack dedication, which leaves you unprepared to play your best. Likewise, you can be highly committed to playing well, but lack the drive to have healthy practice habits.

COMMITMENT TO THE GAME OF GOLF

Your commitment to golf is influenced by several factors. These include: (1) enjoyment of the game; (2) opportunities to play; (3) your physical and emotional stake in the game,; and (4) the priority of golf in your life and its relationship to your involvement in other activities. The more you enjoy the game of golf the more you will continue to play and work on your game. The more opportunities you have to play, the easier it is to stay involved. Having enough time, a course to play, and the funds to play all help keep you involved in golf.

Your physical and emotional investment in the game also modifies your loyalty to golf. The more time and energy you invest in playing, the harder it is to withdraw from the game. Playing golf becomes "addictive." Lastly, your involvement in other activities influences your commitment to golf. If you're fortunate enough to play golf for a living, your priority is golf and you don't have as many competing activities as the amateur golfer does. If you are an amateur golfer, other activities such as work, school, or other sports take greater precedence over golf. The nature of some careers don't allow for some people to play as often as they would like. The more sports you play, the less time you have for golf.

You can change most of these areas to increase your commitment to golf, but your dedication ultimately depends on the priority of golf in your life. Increasing your enjoyment of golf is a good place to start. This is something that can be done without affecting other areas in your life. You also can establish more opportunities to play by finding more time to play and having the facilities to play and practice. As you begin to play and practice more, you will naturally increase your emotional investment in the game.

The last area that may be the most difficult to modify, especially for amateurs, is the activities that compete with golf. Changing other activities depends on how much emphasis you place on golf in your life. Modifying your investment in other activities depends on your dedication and commitment to these alternative activities. For the serious golfer, it is easy to make the decision to play more golf and fewer alternative sports. For the occasional golfer, it is hard to justify abandoning other pursuits to become a better golfer. Thus, you

164

have to think about your priorities in life and where golf fits, and then make the adjustments in other activities that fits your personal investment in golf.

COMMITMENT TO IMPROVING YOUR MENTAL GAME

Throughout this book, I have discussed the importance of the mental game of golf for achieving peak performance. To get the most out of your game you have to eliminate ineffective ways of thinking, and develop mental toughness and the ability to cope in pressure situations. Not only is it important to continue to develop your ball striking and shot making, but you also have to commit yourself to refining your mental skills. As I stressed in Chapter 8, mental skills are similar to physical skills—they take time to develop.

Don't expect that just reading a technique or suggestion in this book is going to make you a complete mentally tough player. Most players, in the absence of mental training through the years, have acquired bad patterns of thinking and behaving. These ineffective ways of thinking are deeply ingrained and have become habits. Habits take a long time to break and positive change doesn't happen overnight. Don't expect immediate, long-term change without making a commitment to yourself to work on changing your mental game over the long haul.

Everyone can become a mentally tough player as long as they apply themselves to improving mental skills, and if they play enough to understand how they think and react in competition. A good place to start is in practice, but eventually you have to learn to think and behave well under pressure in competition. The more times you put yourself in a situation that requires you to use your mental resources the easier it is to deal with that situation the next time.

> **One thing I know from experience is that the more times you play in pressure situations, the more you'll improve at performing in them.**
> *Curtis Strange (1990), PGA Tour*

Practice your skills on and off the golf course, but test the progress you are making by playing in as many tournaments as you can. The more you expose yourself to competitive pressures and trying situations during tournaments, the faster you will acquire the mental skills that will help you play relaxed and reach peak performance more often. Every day, every week, and every year present a different challenge to your mental game. Each time you play, look forward to encountering a new challenge that tests your mental strength. Commit yourself to mastering the mental game of golf and you will come closer to reaching your full potential as a player.

CHAPTER SUMMARY

• The nature of the game presents special challenges for the golfer. The amount of downtime between shots, being accountable for your own actions, and trying to perfect an imperfect game tests a golfer's psychological mastery of the game.

• A comfort zone is an expectation about what you think you are capable of shooting. Don't change your aggressive style of play when you begin find yourself playing beyond your expectations— stay with the same game plan. Stay focused on one shot at a time and don't limit yourself with thinking that you are playing over your head.

• Overcoming impatience is a big challenge for all golfers. Impatience makes you change your game plan, gamble more, and try too hard. Remember that impatience only cause you to focus on the past and make poor decisions on the shots to follow. Maintain your composure by putting it behind you and playing in the present.

• Sometimes we become too serious and lose sight of the fun aspects of the game. You have to accept that golf is an imperfect game played by people who are likely to make errors. Keep in mind what you enjoy about the game and make that your goal. Increase your challenge or set a different goal to help you become immersed in the process.

• Finding a balanced level of motivation is a key to achieving peak performance. A lack of motivation causes you to not be willing to work hard enough to be fully prepared. Increase your motivation by focusing more on your goals, making practice more challenging, and working to improve your weaknesses.

• Overmotivation causes you to work too hard, try too hard, and become tense and anxious when playing. Some ways to help you relax include keeping your mind focused in the present, emphasizing the process over the outcome, taking a time out, and accepting your limitations.

• A complete golfer must combine both motivation and commitment to be the best he can be. You can increase your commitment to golf, but it depends on how high a priority golf is in your life. Commitment to enhancing your mental approach to the game is very important for long-term change. Bad habits take a long time to change. Learning to master your mental skills is a never-ending process.

REFERENCES

Alcott, A., & Wade, D. (1991). *Amy Alcott's Guild to Women's Golf.* Penguin Books USA Inc.: New York, N.Y.

Azinger, P. (1991). "A Word to the Wise About How-to Articles." *Golf World*, Vol 45 (11). p. 36.

Ballesteros, S. & Andrisani, J. (1988). *Natural Golf.* Macmillan Publishing: New York.

Cohn, P.J. (1991). "An exploratory study on peak performance in golf." *The Sport Psychologist.* 5, 1-14.

Cohn, P.J. (1993). *The Mental Game of Golf: Perspectives from Tour Pros.* Unpublished manuscript. University of North Texas, Denton, TX.

Dorman, L. (December, 1992). "Dialogue on Golf: Greg Norman." *Golf Digest*, 42 (12). pp. 158-179.

Ferguson, H. (1972). *The Edge.* Getting the Edge, Co.: Cleveland, OH.

Gallwey, T. (1979). *The Inner Game of Golf.* Random House: New York, N.Y.

Graham, D. (1990). *Mental Toughness Training for Golf.* Stephen Green-Pellham Books: New York, N.Y.

Hogan, B. (1957). *Five Lessons: The Modern Fundamentals of Golf.* Simon & Schuster: New York, N.Y.

Kite, T. (November, 1993). "I'll Make You a Better Player." *Golf Digest*, Vol 44 (1), p. 55.

Kite, T. & Dennis, L. (1990). *How to Play Consistent Golf.* Golf Digest/Tennis Inc.: Trumbull, CT.

Lopez, N., & Wade, D. (1987). *Nancy Lopez's The Complete Golfer.* Contemporary Books: Chicago, IL.

Nicklaus, J. & Bowden, K. (1974). *Golf My Way.* Simon & Schuster: New York, N.Y.

Norman, G., & Peper, G. (1988). *Shark Attack! Greg Norman's Guide to Aggressive Golf*. Simon & Schuster: New York, N.Y.

Norman, G., & Peper, G. (1993). *Greg Norman's Instant Lessons*. Simon & Schuster: New York, N.Y.

Trevino, L. (1992). CNBC. *The Dick Cavett Show*. June 17, 1992.

Van Sickle, G. (March, 1990). "Normal Norman." *Golf World*, Vol 43, (33), 12-16.

ABOUT THE AUTHOR

Dr. Patrick J. Cohn received his Ph.D. from the University of Virginia in sports psychology. His studies focused on the psychology of golf and applying sports psychology techniques to golf, especially preshot routines in golf, an area in which he is considered a leading expert. His research in sports psychology includes studies on preshot routines, peak performance, self-confidence, the psychology of putting, and stress and burnout in golf. Dr. Cohn has taught classes in sports psychology and motor learning at the University of Virginia, Miami University of Ohio, and the University of North Texas. Dr. Cohn consults with several professional golfers on the PGA, LPGA, Nike, and Asian Tours. He also has consulted extensively with collegiate and amateur players for the last seven years. In addition to being an eight handicap golfer, Dr. Cohn plays tennis and racquetball. Presently, Dr. Cohn is the head of Peak Performance Consultants, a consulting firm that helps professional, collegiate, and recreational athletes achieve maximum performance and enhance personal growth. To contact Dr. Cohn write:

Dr. Patrick J. Cohn
Peak Performance Consultants
2706 South Horseshoe Drive • Suite 106
Naples, Florida 33942
(813) 649-1088